For Cooper,

**Without your little hands picking out a book,
daddy would have never written this.
For you buddy, love you!**

Confederate Black Ops: The Untold Story of the Confederate Clandestine Services

by Charles L Tilton II

Copyright © 2015 Author

ISBN 978-0-9895513-3-5
Printed in the United States of America

Published by Blacksmith LLC
Fayetteville, NC

www.BlacksmithPublishing.com

Direct inquiries and/or orders to the above web address.

Contents

Introduction

"It was not well to drive men into final corners; at those moments they could all develop teeth and claws."
– Stephen Crane

Chronicling Civil War intelligence activities can be rather daunting. This is due not only to the paucity of information, but to the questionable truth of some records as well. Complicating everything, it's a well-known fact that the Confederacy's Secretary of State, Judah P. Benjamin, consigned to the flame all the intelligence records he could find as federal troops were entering Richmond. As I'm writing this, the days are drawing near to the 150th Anniversary of the end of the American Civil War, or War of Northern Aggression. And yet most of what we know regarding the Civil War even today pertains to either famous battles – Antietam, Gettysburg, or Averasboro – or famous people – Stuart, Mosby, Grant, or Lee. However, many stories remain untold; shrouded in mystery.

This book is an attempt to shed light on the enormous contribution of one such mysterious entity which in innovative ways fought to preserve the constitutional rights of its fellow Southern citizens. This was the Confederate Secret Service Bureau and Signal Corps. Though special operation units and clandestine operations have become the rage the world over, they are nothing new to American history. Long before there were any special operations units such as the Underwater Demolition Teams (UDT), Ranger Battalions, Jedburgh Detachments, or Office of Strategic Services (OSS),

Introduction

there existed a special operations branch which encapsulated the Confederate Secret Service, Secret Navy, and Special and Detached Services and Signal Corps. These three comprised the covert fighting ability of the Confederacy. Of all the other special operations entities that were created to establish 'a better state of the peace' that had previously existed, none other made such a massive contribution to the war effort. This is what this book hopes to acknowledge and elaborate on.

Little is known and understood about the Confederate Signal Corps and Secret Service Bureau, and even less about how influential the clandestine operations they conducted were or how far reaching their involvement was in the conventional side of the war. Undoubtedly its mysterious nature has caused it to be unsung and unheard, eclipsed by the flamboyancy of a Jeb Stuart or John Singleton Mosby. Likewise, the actions of "Southern gentry," such as the celebrated Robert E. Lee, claim center stage, while the history of the Confederate Signal Corps and Secret Service Bureau occupies a forgotten wing.

There's a great deal of speculation regarding what the Signal Corps and Secret Service Bureau actually did during the war. Were these individuals sanctioned by the Confederate government? How about their clandestine operations? Was there a direct correlation between the Secret Service Bureau and the Lincoln conspirators? An affirmative "yes" is easier to speculate than to actually demonstrate with facts that help support the truth.

In an effort to shed more light on the enormous contributions made by this covert agency, the perspective taken in this book is from an array of aspects. That is, not just the conventional but

Introduction

special operations perspective as well. A perspective, that in my honest opinion, previous historians have neglected to use. Additionally, the vast array of scholarship on this subject centers mainly on the Lincoln assassination but has failed to comprehensibly connect all the pieces; a deficit this work will attempt to rectify. Likewise, it's not a book on conspiracy, but one which places a high premium on facts.

Further, this book will highlight the innovation and ingenuity of this covert agency. Theirs was truly an experimental and complex network. An intelligence and espionage service that was technically and tactically born of its time albeit born before its time; its far-reaching influence felt even today. For whereas the Union's Bureau of Military Information, operated for specific generals, the Confederacy's Secret Service Bureau centralized its activities, thereby, serving as a catalyst for an idea that would eventually become a centralized military intelligence division. As we all know, winners write the history, but what if the losing side was finally able to shed some light on the subject. You decide.

Chapter 1
Creation of the Confederate Secret Service Bureau and Signal Corps

"I say, Captain, do you hear something?"
– Peter Pan

There was much deliberation and arguing, even bloody fighting within the halls of the congressional chambers on Capitol Hill. All of this was occurring mainly because, with the possibility of Abraham Lincoln being elected the new President of the United States, Southerners began to plan and brace themselves for a possible separation from their cousins of the North. During the fragile period just before the war, Southern members of Congress, sensing an ever-growing ostracism, were compelled to decide where their loyalties lay. It was during this crucial period in which many Southern gentry, senators or congressmen in Washington, began laying the foundational architecture of the Confederate Signal Corps and Secret Service Bureau. These individuals had a great deal of access and knowledge of the US military, and began to gather intelligence, securing it for future use. Most of these architects were from border States, making logical sense, because they were the closest to the action and would be able to get the most up to date accounts of intelligence which is what was needed to win a war.

There's a great deal of debate regarding who *really* established the Confederate Secret Service Bureau

and Signal Corps. However, before this is addressed
there are some more important pressing issues. To
begin with, when writing about this area of American
history, historians will normally use certain technical
terms, while not really understanding them.

Likewise, whenever one discusses covert
operations, there is even more difficultly. Perhaps
this is due to a disparity between civilian and
military terms. Therefore, in order to limit confusion
and foster a better understanding of what these
individuals did, a short discussion of technical
terminology is necessary.

First of all, it must be understood that if one is
speaking of anything having to do with military
operations, then the military terminology is therefore
the prepotency. With that in mind, here are some
terms we need to be familiar with: **unconventional
warfare**, **irregular warfare**, and **guerilla warfare.**
Although these terms are often used sparingly, being
quite foreign in the verbiage of the modern world,
they are essential to gaining an understanding of the
complexities involved with a study of a subject such
as covert operations. Further, as will be seen, there's
a clear distinction between each of the before
mentioned topics.

First, **Guerrilla warfare** is defined as, *operations
conducted in an enemy-held or hostile territory by
irregular,* **predominantly** *indigenous forces.*[1] Could it
be argued that some of the members of the
Confederate Signal Corps and Secret Service Bureau

---

[1] Department of the Army, *FM 1-02 (FM 101-5-1) Operational Terms
and Graphics*, (Washington D.C.: Headquarters Department of the
Army, 2004), 1-90.

were the "indigenous force"? Yes, this could be argued and tactfully constituted. However, an *insurgency movement aimed at the overthrow of a* **constituted government** *through use of subversion and armed conflict* is also an underlying part, but then again were there really **predominantly** *indigenous forces* at work or was it foreign nationals leading a revolt against another government entity?[2] Questions such as that need to be considered and will be answered for clarification not just speculation.

The next term overused is *unconventional warfare* and if and when the Confederate Signal Corps and Secret Service Bureau used this method of warfare. **Unconventional Warfare (UW)** is defined as, *activities conducted to enable a* **resistance movement or insurgency** *to coerce, disrupt, or overthrow a government or occupying power by operating through or with an underground, auxiliary, and guerrilla force in a denied area.* [3] Now the Confederate Secret Service Bureau and Signal Corps were masters in this form of craft, because they were attempting *to coerce and disrupt an occupying power.* Therefore, from the moment of inception, they were conducting **irregular warfare methods** because they were *armed individuals or groups who are not members of the regular armed forces, police, or other internal security forces.*[4]

---

[2] JP-305.

[3] Ibid.

[4] Department of the Army, *FM 1-02 (FM 101-5-1) Operational Terms and Graphics*, 1-105.

Again they could be considered an internal
security force, and this is agreeable to an extent.
However, they were also an external security force,
such as *Mosby's Rangers for example,* who ranged
vast areas of enemy occupied land. There will be
more about this in subsequent chapters.

Two other words that are commonly misconstrued
are **sabotage** and **subversion;** if the latter is even
used at all. **Sabotage** is, *"an act or acts with intent
to injure, interfere with, or obstruct the **national
defense of a country** by willfully injuring or
destroying, or attempting to injure or destroy any
national defense or war materiel, premises, or utilities,
to include human and natural resources".*[5] Nowhere
in this definition are civilians the primary "target" of
the operation and this is where **subversion** comes
into play; which is defined as an, *"action designed to
undermine the military, economic, psychological, or
political strength or morale of a regime".* [6]

Finally, to better understand the Confederate
Secret Service Bureau and Signal Corps, we need to
look at three more words: **covert, overt,** and
clandestine. The easiest way to remember what
each of those terms means is as follows: **covert**
refers to an operation undertaken which lacks the
acknowledgement of who did it; **overt** refers to an
operation undertaken that is openly acknowledged,
and lastly, **clandestine** refers to an operation
undertaken in which there is no acknowledgement
that "it" ever happened.

---

[5] Department of the Army, *FM 1-02 (FM 101-5-1) Operational Terms
and Graphics*, 1-105, 1-165.

[6] Ibid, 1-178.

Chapter 1 Creation of the Confederate Secret Service Bureau and Signal Corps

"If you call one wolf, you invite the pack."
– Bulgarian Proverb

Regarding the development of the Confederate Secret Service Bureau and Signal Corps, though most historians, even the everyday history aficionado, look to the first actions taken by the Confederate Congress in 1864. What they often overlook is the fact that it began without congressional approval; much like men have known to do throughout history. Foremost in the development of the Confederate Bureau of Special and Secret Service, a man who should be regarded as the first known recruiter, was Governor John Letcher of Virginia.

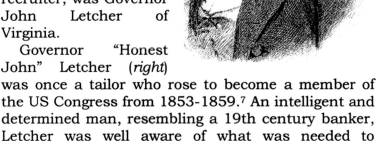

Governor "Honest John" Letcher (*right*) was once a tailor who rose to become a member of the US Congress from 1853-1859.[7] An intelligent and determined man, resembling a 19th century banker, Letcher was well aware of what was needed to

---

[7] John Letcher (1813-1884), was a journalist, a lawyer and later a politician. He served as a Representative in the US Congress, and was the 34th Governor of the State of Virginia during the American Civil War.

produce an effective intelligence network.[8] And by December 1860, South Carolina had already passed a resolution to leave the Union and it was assumed that many, if not all, the Southern States would follow her lead in the very near future.[9]

Sensing that his home State of Virginia would readily follow suit, Letcher set up his very own intelligence gathering network in Washington, in preparation for a war with the Northern States. Further, Letcher knew that he must have his "inside man" to get the process underway, one that was not only intelligent, but able to recruit and train others for future operations.

Letcher's choice, a man who fit all of these qualifications was Thomas Jordon, a West Point graduate, and active duty officer. Thomas Jordan lost no time recruiting intelligence collectors in Washington. This was during the later months of 1860 when folks met in various locations throughout the nation's capital; some pro-Union, others separatist. For the later, one such meeting location was Mr. Beach's livery stable, which was within the confines of Washington. It was there that Letcher's recruiters often gathered to meet. A primary recruiter at Mr. Beach's was known simply as *Doctor B__*. To his potential recruits, Doctor B__ was very vocal as

---

[8] Vera Palmer, *"Honest John' Letcher, War Governor From Tailor's Bench to Old Dominion's Executive Mansion Is Romance of Little Known, Much Loved Virginian."* Richmond Times-Dispatch (Richmond, VA), January 13, 1935.

[9] Philip Van Doren Stern, *Secret Missions of the Civil War,* (New York: Bonanza Books, 1987), 37.

to who his supporter was – *Honest John.*[10] More will follow on Doctor B__ and what he was aiming to do in a subsequent chapter. An important note in all of this is that Governor Letcher conducted all these actions prior to May 1861; single handedly. The point being made here is the architect of the Confederate Secret Service Bureau and Signal Corps was none other than Letcher. He made the preparations, laid the cornerstone, and understood what was at stake; not Thomas Jordan or any other individual. None the less, this was all conducted by a concerned civilian, political leader, and Southerner.

A man concerned with the preservation of the constitutional rights of his fellow Southern citizens. A man who sought a better state of the peace (s*i vis pacem, para bellum*).

Captain William Norris *(left)*, the first Confederate government official to head the Confederate Secret Service Bureau and Signal Corps, took command of the Confederate Signal Corps on 29 May, 1862 by General Order #40, and on 31 July, 1862 was ordered to Richmond to serve as the bureau chief.[11] William Norris was an interesting character in the whole story of the Confederate Secret Service and

---

[10] Van Doren Stern, 37-43.

[11] William Norris (1820-1896).

Signal Corps; having been born in Baltimore County, Maryland a free state with Southern sympathies. He was a Yale College graduate (Class of 1840), a forty-niner in California, practiced law in New Orleans, served as the Judge Advocate to the US Navy Pacific Squadron, and served as president for the Baltimore Mechanical Bakery.[12]

There were strong Pro-Confederacy feelings about Baltimore during the winter of 1860-61; and Norris was an individual that had the same feelings. He took his family to Richmond, VA and was given the job of establishing a system of signals, based on what he had witnessed during his time as the Judge Advocate for the United States Navy. Impressed with what Norris had done, Brigadier General John Bankhead Magruder recommended Norris be granted a commission as a Captain in the Confederate Army by way of a letter to the Confederate Secretary of War. It took some time, but eventually Norris was commissioned as a signal officer and later as Major Norris, he would head the organization and implementation of the Confederate Secret Service Bureau and Signal Corps.

It is time to address the difference between the Signal Corps and the Secret Service Bureau. The Confederate Signal Corps was the first of the two to be created and its sole purpose was the signal aspect of the Confederate War Department; whereas the Secret Service Bureau (SSB) consisted of the *clandestine operatives* of the Confederacy. The Signal Corps was instrumental in all signal aspects to

---

[12] David Winfred Gaddy, "William Norris - and the Confederate Signal and Secret Service," last modified January 1, 2014, http://mdscv.org/1398/Norrisbio.htm.

include: telegraph wiretapping, signal flags, signals for the blockade runners, ciphers for agents and dignitaries, and the communication lines that the Confederacy used throughout not only the United States but Canada, Mexico and Europe. The Signal Corps also encompasses the Special and Detached Services (SDS). The SDS was responsible for the Baltimore and Washington City agents. They compiled intelligence that was collected by these agents and passed this information on to the Confederate War Department.

The SSB is the basis of all the great flamboyant individuals of the Confederate military; and yet at the same time the most controversial. There is a great deal of finger pointing as to the action(s) this group played in the assassination of President Lincoln. That is, were they mere rouges or did they execute the directives of the Confederate Government? Many historians fail to link the two offices together, as well as the Confederate Department of the Navy, which played a pivotal role in the operations conducted by the other groups; as well as other agencies that operated as splinter cells of the three.

The diagram (Figure 1) is an attempt to graphically demonstrate how the first levels of the cells were linked directly to President Jefferson Davis *(Executive Branch)*; and thus linking all the different cells and organizations together. This is where the previously mentioned controversy is derived from; one can argue speculation but cannot argue facts. The Confederate Signal Corps and Secret Service Bureau were not born of necessity but were derived purely from fear and speculation; which surprisingly was advantageous to the Confederate government in the future of the nation.

> ***"I'm making perfect sense, you're just not keeping up."***
> *– Doctor Who*

How each of these groups, cells, units, or organizations correlate with each other is a puzzling complexity; one which needs to be explained up front, which we now move on to do. The Confederate Department of the Navy (DON), SSB, and SDS and Signal Corps often, if not regularly, used the same cells to develop their intelligence packages and message traffic.

Stephen R. Mallory, having served in the US Senate as well as the chairman of the Committee of Naval Affairs, made him the perfect choice for Secretary of the Confederate Navy. In this post, Mallory was able to give breath to the Secret Navy which was headed up by James Dunwoody Bulloch. [13] The Secret Navy was then connected to the *Richmond Line,* aka Secret Line, Maryland Line or Doctor Line, a courier service that was set up by George N. Sanders. [14] The Richmond Line passed information to and from the Canadian Bureau; which

---

[13] James Tertuis de Kay, *The Rebel Raiders: The Astonishing History of the Confederacy's Secret Navy,* (New York: The Random House Publishing Group, 2002), 14.

[14] "Intelligence in the Civil War," *cia.gov,* last modified January 03, 2012 at https://www.cia.gov/library/publications/additional-publications/civil-war/p5.htm.

was passing information obtained via the *Richmond Line* or to the *Richmond Line* from the Secret Service Fund (SSF). The SSF then reported its intelligence to the Confederate War Department, same as the Department of the Navy (DON). However, the *Richmond Line* fell under the direct command of the Secret Service Bureau; as did the Polytechnic Corps that was under the Confederate DON as well (see Figure 1).

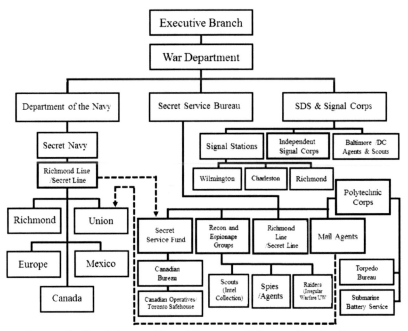

Figure 1. Confederate Signal Corps and Secret Service Bureau
Link Analysis.

It is understood that Maj. Norris was the officer in charge of the Confederate Secret Service Bureau, Special Detached Service and Signal Corps.

However, his executive officer (XO), Captain William
N. Barker is noted as, *"Captain in charge of the signal
corps in July 1863".*[15] The two are mentioned as one,
so as not to cause confusion. However, it is believed,
and makes perfect sense, that the Special and
Detached Service was really the cover for the Secret
Service Bureau. This was a cleaver attempt to clearly
acknowledge that the Confederacy had a signal unit,
while it disguised their intelligence collection and
operations detachment (Secret Service Bureau). This
conclusion is strengthened by the fact that each time
the Confederate Congress met on any matter
concerning the two it was under a secret session.

The Confederacy's ability to keep their operational
unit as hush as possible kept them ahead of the
game against the Union forces that were ill-equipped
to handle or keep up with them. Here it may be seen
that the Confederacy's Secret Service Bureau
centralized its activities, and unlike their Northern
opponents, created a covert military intelligence
gathering agency. The units that branched off of the
SDS and Signal Corps were the various signal
stations, and to note: Wilmington, Charleston and
Richmond; as well as the Independent Signal Corps
(which was formed through jealousy), and lastly the
Baltimore and Washington City agents and scouts
(see Figure 1).

The SDS and Signal Corps operated independently
from the Secret Service Bureau. This organizational
structure caused much chaos due primarily to the
unwillingness of many in command to work together,
seeing themselves as superior. The organizational
chart shows the SDS, Signal Corps, and Secret

---

[15] David Winfred Gaddy.

Chapter 1 Creation of the Confederate Secret Service Bureau and Signal Corps

Service Bureau as separate entities; their own operational units. This is because they actually were separate in reality; but to cover the truth behind the Secret Service Bureau, Major Norris has been known to be listed as the commander of the SDS and Signal Corps on paper. This act caused confusion for the Union as much to anyone researching or reading about the organizations. What this would do is allow the enemy to draw conclusions that the Secret Service Bureau was a part of or branched off of the SDS and Signal Corps when in all actuality it did not. However, perception is reality.

When researching the Secret Service Bureau, it was a complex web of various units that conducted just about every task during war time; with information on each in different areas but lacking organization to each. This is the first known link analysis chart or flow chart of the Secret Service Bureau, to mind. The various units had to have some sort of organization to function as effectively as each did; however those wanting to move up the chain of command did hinder the operations and successes of some units and the intelligence that was passed on. The following are the sub-units of the Secret Service Bureau: Secret Service Fund (SSF), Recon and Espionage Groups, Richmond Line, Mail Agents, and Polytechnic Corps *(the breakdown of each when noted can also be found in Figure 1)*.

It has been said that the Secret Service Fund, under the command of Captain Thomas Henry Hines, was organized to conduct sabotage operations.[16] However, it must be noted that their operations included subversion in conjunction with

---

[16] "Intelligence in the Civil War", 43.

sabotage as well. The Secret Service Fund was at the top of the pyramid. It was followed directly by the Canadian Bureau which had units branch off such as the Northwest Confederacy, the Operation Stations which were located in Halifax, Quebec City, Niagara, Toronto, Montreal, and Nova Scotia; and lastly the Canadian Operatives and main safe house.

The Recon and Espionage Groups were broken down into three sub units; the scouts (collected intelligence mainly on the battlefield), the spies (worked within the confines of the more populated areas), and the raiders (that conducted irregular warfare methods as well as unconventional warfare). As previously mentioned, the *Richmond Line* served other entities or units but fell under the Secret Service Bureau command structure. The main stops that were traveled on the line were: Richmond, Baltimore, Newfoundland, England, France, Spain, and lastly, Mexico. The second to last unit that falls under the Secret Service Bureau's command are the mail agents. This group of agents collected open source material from the Union. This intelligence in turn could be used to aid the Confederate Army. A covert mail system, developed by Texan John H. Reagan, contained hidden messages in the personal columns. These newspapers normally hailed from Maryland.[17]

One final covert unit, the Polytechnic Corps, was organized under H.R. 361 of the Confederate Congress on 6 March, 1865 by secret session. [18]

---

[17] "Intelligence in the Civil War", 13.

[18] Doug Linder, "The Trial of the Lincoln Assassination Conspirators," last modified January 1, 2009,

Chapter 1 Creation of the Confederate Secret Service Bureau and Signal Corps

Though this House Resolution was at the end of war, it is understood, however, that the units that would fall under this corps were well in place and active before this resolution went before the congress. The two units under this corps were the Torpedo Bureau under the command of Brigadier General Gabriel Rains [19] , and the Submarine Battery Service commanded by Captain Matthew Fontaine Maury[20]. These two units were some of the few that actually worked together in unison, and were successful because one created the torpedo and the other the *CSS Hunley* which made naval history. Most, at least Southerners, have come to fall in love with the honor and awe that surrounds the Hunley, which was not previously linked to the Confederate Secret Service Bureau and Signal Corps. These units conducted various operations throughout the world, and now there is a link between each entity and where it laid in the entire spectrum.

With an organizational apparatus in place to conduct covert warfare, the Confederacy's Secret Service Bureau was more than just a band of miscreants refusing to side with the Union, but rather geniuses that changed history, by creating a

---

http://law2.umkc.edu/faculty/projects/ftrials/lincolnconspiracy/lincolnaccount.html.

[19] "The Confederacy's Bomb Brothers," National Mine Action Center Issue 6.1, jmu.edu, last modified April 2002, http://www.jmu.edu/cisr/journal/6.1/notes/robbins/robbins.htm.

[20] R.O. Crowley, "*The Confederate Torpedo Service,*" The Century Illustrated Monthly Magazine, Volume 56 (1898): 290.

Chapter 1 Creation of the Confederate Secret Service Bureau and Signal Corps

covert military intelligence gathering agency – the first of its kind.

Having discussed the organizational framework of the Confederacy's Secret Service Bureau, it may be viewed that this was quite a complex network that was developed throughout the war, leaving many questions begging answers. Thus, what had begun as Letcher's tight-knit fledging intelligence agency on the banks of the Potomac, grew into a perplexing, enigma of almost mythical proportions by war's end.

Chapter 2
Trust Bearer

"Coming together is a beginning; keeping together is progress; working together is success."
– Henry Ford

Although officially established by the Confederate Congress in 1864, as we've seen, this covert agency didn't begin there, but rather much earlier. The birth of this organization began when Southern sympathizers set in place independent intelligence collection and defense networks. These were not individuals that were seeking to overthrow the American government or destroy it, but to stand up for their rights as defended by the United States Constitution. Men such as Governor John Letcher were such individuals. What is commonly missed in any discussion of this nature is what he did and the operatives he recruited. As we've seen, Letcher was in fact the first intelligence network recruiter and handler for the Southern cause. This man was extremely influential and was able to rally many different individuals to form his own coterie.

The first chapter gave insight of how this organization came to be, the *Virginia Society*. This organization included what is referred to as the *Greenhow Group* and the *National Volunteers;* both of which were in existence because of Letcher, and why it should be referred to as the *Virginia Society*. Plus, this society also included those agents from Baltimore and the State of Maryland, the Doctor Line, and Virginia agents. There is a great deal of credit given to Rose Greenhow for what she was able to accomplish, and rightfully so. However, as is being argued, the man that created it all is left out of the mix and is never given full credit for what he did. Perhaps it's easier for historians to glamorize attractive females then balding, hefty, middle aged politicians. In point of fact, it was Letcher who was the actual ring master, without whom, inarguably, the Confederate Secret Service and Signal Corps would not have existed. And the man who enacted Letcher's great scheme was Thomas Jordan. However, before we discuss how Letcher stood up this covert agency by way of Thomas Jordan, a short discussion of its organization must follow.

To put it all into perspective, the Virginia Society became the Signal Corps, the Maryland and Doctor Line became the Richmond Line, and the various agents were absorbed into these new organizations as well as the Secret Service Bureau and its supplement detachments. The Virginia Society was perfectly organized as an **underground** element, because *it was a covert unconventional warfare organization that was established to operate in areas denied to the guerrilla forces or conduct operations not suitable for guerilla forces;* as well as an **auxiliary**, which was the *element of the resistance forces established to provide the organized civilian support of the resistance movement.*[21] This will be broken down into detail in this chapter; but to skip ahead the agents were the *underground,* and the couriers / safe houses the *auxiliary* (see diagram).

---

[21] Department of the Army, *FM 1-02 (FM 101-5-1) Operational Terms and Graphics*, 1-193.

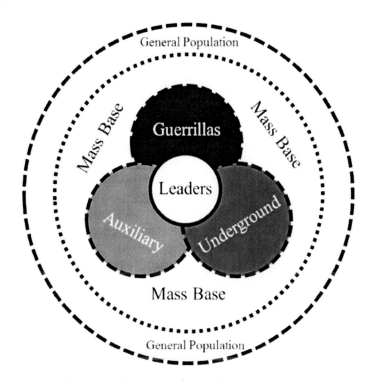

Figure 2. Elements of a Resistance Movement.

*"Believe only half of what you see
and nothing that you hear."*
– Edgar Allan Poe

Thomas Jordan was born on 30 September, 1819 in Luray, VA to a family born to serve in defense of the nation he held allegiance to; as well as being directly related to the former George Washington helped in the direct development of his cavaliering persona.[22]

---

[22] William J. Marrin, "Thomas Jordan," June 11th, 1896, last Modified November 27, 2010,

Thomas Jordan (below) was the main individual that was entrusted to lead the intelligence detachment of the Virginia Society, the other was a  man known as Doctor B__. Doctor B__ was affiliated with the *National Rifles*, and to be exact there is great speculation that he was the *shadow commanding officer* of this organization. The National Rifles started out as an organized Union militia unit whose purpose was to quell any rebellion that may form, thereby protecting Washington City. The National Rifles was essentially a company-sized infantry element that was supplied with arms from the Washington Arsenal. The secessionist members that broke away from its ranks joined the sister pro-Southern company named the *National Volunteers*.

Interestingly enough, there was an early plot in January 1861, backed by Gov. Letcher, to capture Washington City by way of these two militia organizations. This was to prevent the inauguration of President Elect-Lincoln. How close the National Rifles and National Volunteers were in accomplishing this act remains a mystery. There are many *"what ifs"* during the War of Northern Aggression concerning the Confederacy and this is one of those. Captain Charles S. Schaeffer was the recruiting officer and commanding officer of the National Rifles,

http://penelope.uchicago.edu/Thayer/E/Gazetteer/Places/America/United_States/Army/USMA/AOG_Reunions/27/Thomas_Jordan*.html.

and was very adamant that the reason for their consistent drilling and training was to keep the Union forces from making their way to the South via Maryland.

What was even more shocking is that no one was aware of the militia unit's true intent under the command of her officers. Furthermore, the unit was provided with arms and munitions from a direct order to the Chief of Ordnance from the then Secretary of War John B. Floyd of Virginia. The order read that, *"...all ordnance and ordnance stores that he (Cpt. Schaeffer) might require for his company!"* While Captain Schaeffer was organizing men for his legitimate militia, Doctor B__ was organizing the *National Volunteers* and served as its commanding officer. This military unit met at Beach's livery stable nightly for preparations to seize Washington City. While forming under the false pretense that they were answering the Union's call to defend the capital, they were all the while waiting for the notification to seize the capital. Unwittingly, the US government would then provide them with the same armament as the National Rifles. The question now is who was to give this notification, and what authority did this individual have?

It can be concluded that the notification would have come from Gov. Letcher, because he was the primary supporter of the *National Volunteers*. The members of the National Volunteers debated on which buttons should be requested for their newly voted on gray uniforms. The chosen button was that of the State of Maryland *(remember Maryland was a major Southern sympathizing state, thus in favor of state buttons)* and not the American Eagle buttons. Although the majority of the members were

21

immensely in favor of the state buttons to signify the support of Southern state rights; many concerned this might cause eyebrows to raise that they were secessionist. They wanted to keep the "target" off their back until the time was right, and incarceration by Unionist was not part of the plan.

Doctor B__ assured the men of the National Volunteers that the Gov. of Virginia would ensure that they were equipped properly. The election of the officers was required before the Doctor could properly equip his men. And after being carried by a vote, Doctor B__ was to serve as the commanding officer. Tableting his new unit's needs, the Doctor hand delivered his requisition to the Inspector General Charles P. Stone, who unbeknownst to the Doctor and Schaeffer, was actively collecting on the two men, and had in fact inserted an operative. The Doctor was unaware that he would not receive the arms that he requested. Immediately following Doctor B__ was Captain Schaeffer's requisition for more arms that were to be provided via the order from Secretary of War Floyd. The inspector General Charles P. Stone flatly denied Schaeffer's request, telling him that he had more than enough necessary arms. The infuriated Captain Schaeffer, piqued from such a refusal, threatened to take the nearby Columbian Armory by force and stormed out of the inspector's office.

By the time Schaeffer reached his office, he received an order to turn in all of his arms, and not having enough time to round up enough men to resist, he followed the order.[23] If Captain Schaeffer had not made such a threat, it is presumed that he would have been able to keep his company's arms,

---

[23] Van Doren Stern, 37-43.

and those could have been transferred over to the Confederate forces. However, the greediness of the captain got to him, and the personal connections that he once held did not hold up anymore under a new regime. The pro-South men of Captain Schaeffer's Company joined forces with that of Doctor B__'s. These men joined the Alexandria Battalion of the Virginia Volunteers. This man known only as **Doctor B__** in the history books was actually **Major Cornelius Boyle** who had been a very successful physician in Washington City prior to the hostilities. He was to command the men that he helped organize a month prior, but turned it down to become the provost marshal of Manassas.[24]

> **"So this is how liberty dies**
> **– with thunderous applause.**
> *– Padmé Amidala*

The Southern states were beginning to leave the Northern states one by one; and the North was calling up men to destroy the rebellion quickly. The freedom of the States to govern themselves was destroyed the moment President Lincoln called men to arms, as were the civil liberties that the people of the once *United* States of America cherished and held in high regard. The first official confrontation would be the Battle of First Manassas; and the intelligence

---

[24] William A. Tidwell, *April '65: Confederate Covert Action in the American Civil War,* (Kent, OH: The Kent State University, 1995), 63.

–By reading and comparing various texts I concluded that Doctor B__ was Major Boyle. I have yet to find any other book, manuscript, etc., that has also come to this conclusion by linking.

collected was pivotal, and would decide who would be on the winning side.

The line of agents that were recruited and trained by their respective handler showed the leadership in Richmond just how significant they really were. Thomas Jordan was a veteran of two different military actions, the Seminole Indian War and the Mexican War, and this made him a very sought after individual. The segment below is from Jordan's obituary from the United States Military Academy, and shows what an amazing an innovative soldier he was:

Thomas Jordan graduated West Point in 1840, one of his class-mates and room-mate being William Tecumseh Sherman. He entered service at once in the Infantry, and early distinguished himself during the Seminole uprising in Florida, 1841 to 1843. During a portion of this period he was the adjutant of his regiment, acting later as assistant adjutant-general of a military district. While still a lieutenant, he served with his regiment in the Mexican War, taking part in the battles of Palo Alto and Resaca de la Palma. His company, with three others, constituted the first battalion to cross the Rio Grande, as a cover to the crossing of General Taylor's whole army into Mexico.

Later he was selected for a captaincy on the general staff, was assigned to the Quartermaster's Department and stationed at Vera Cruz, the base of operations of General Scott, from which the army drew its supplies in the campaign which ended in the conquest of Mexico. He had finally charge of all the Quartermaster's arrangements for the evacuation of Mexico, owing to the illness of his senior, and in this was included the sea and land transportation of 35,000 men, in completion of which Captain Jordan was the last American soldier to leave the soil of Mexico. His efficiency in this service was specially mentioned by General Twiggs, the Commander at Vera Cruz, to the Quartermaster-General at Washington.

Chapter 2 Trust Bearer

During a second uprising of the Seminoles and their transfer west of the Mississippi, Captain Jordan was in charge of the chief depot of the Quartermaster's staff, until he was assigned in January, 1852, to special duty at Washington City. From August, 1852, to December, 1860, he served as Quartermaster on the Pacific Coast, notably during the skillful operations conducted by Colonel George Wright, for the suppression of a serious widespread Indian insurrection in the present State of Washington. His services received the highest official testimony. The introduction of steam navigation on the Upper Columbia River, above the Dalles, at this time, was his own project and first achieved by him; and the first successful system of irrigation of the arid plains was instigated by him. The former matured into the Oregon Navigation Company. He was well known and esteemed for the intelligent painstaking with which he aided, by the influence of his official station, everything in the nature of legitimate pioneering, as also for the personal friendliness and assistance which he bestowed upon the seemingly worthy among unfortunates.[25]

As can be surmised, Jordan was the perfect man for the job. Additionally, because he was a native Virginian, he was highly desired by Letcher. After he was confronted with Gov. Letcher's offer on the possibility of conducting intelligence gathering operations for him, he began to recruit his own agents to ensure the success of the operations. Jordan formed his own detachment with himself sitting at the head of this intelligence gathering operation. A person he was able to recruit, *and is no stranger to War of Northern Aggression history*, is Rose O'Neal Greenhow.

---

[25] William J. Marrin.

Chapter 2 Trust Bearer

"Because she feels. I don't. All I know is logic."
– Commander Spock

Rose O'Neal Greenhow (1813-1864) was well known within the confines of Washington City during the mid-19th century. Her late husband was once a US government employee working for the State Department. This made her a valuable asset because she knew and understood Washington City as well as the people that enveloped its complicated network and structure. She was known for her beauty, elegance, manners, and politeness which were all attractive to mid-19th century "aristocrats" especially within the nation's capital. Historian Carl Sandburg described her as, *"...a tall, brunet with slumberous eyes...slightly horse-faced, having gaunt beauty, education and manners and resourceful speech."*[26]

How is it known that Greenhow (right) was influential? Well let's take stock of two of her congressional gentleman callers: Senator Joseph Lane, southern Democrat, of Oregon and Senator Henry Wilson, northern Republican of Massachusetts. [27] These two members of the US Senate were at one time presumably willing to divulge information to Greenhow.

---

[26] Merton T. Akers, "Confederate Spy Found Dead", *Reading Eagle*, 26 September 1964.

There is no hard evidence at this time to implicate these two men as agents of Greenhow. However, there is strong opinion, and justifiably so that they were. If one looks at just the facts, perhaps these gentlemen were willing to tell an attractive female information concerning troop movements, etc., which was sensitive in nature especially during a time of war. There is no way, logically, that both of these gentlemen were unaware of Greenhow's dealing and just who she was supporting, and who they were supporting with their loose lips.

Lane was a Southern born Democrat and would inarguably pass on information as he could until his term in office was up in March of 1861. After which time Senator Wilson, who later became the Vice President of the United States of America under Grant, was a member of the Senate Committee on Military Affairs, and more than likely conducted a hand over with Lane. There is much speculation that he passed on various amounts of information to Greenhow as well as love letters signed simply as *"H"*, strangely enough as if referring to Henry; and the letter *(right)* has congressional letterhead, attesting his love to Rose.[28]

---

[27] "Intelligence in the Civil War."

[28] "Rose O'Neal Greenhow - Confederate Spy."

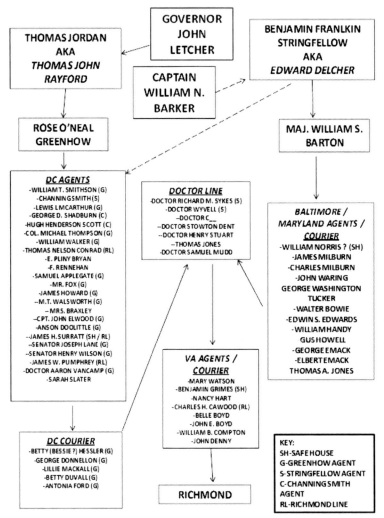

Figure 3: Virginia Society and future Special and Detached Service and Signal Corps flow chart.

To argue against facts simply to save the pride of these men because they were "respectable" men of society is absurd. One man was known to have feelings against the Union, and the other just because he became Vice President of the United States of America. New books have been written implicating another individual in hopes of saving what reputation Wilson still maintains. Now why does any of this matter? It matters because the information that Greenhow **did** receive from Wilson on the troop movements enabled the Confederacy to win the Battle of First Manassas.

There is no logical way that she learned about the troop movements from any other source or open source; the pieces of the puzzle fall into place and Wilson had to have been a Greenhow agent. The complexity on who worked or associated with whom and so forth can be confusing; *Figure 3* breaks it down in a flow / link chart format.

"Men willingly believe what they wish."
– Julius Caesar

The Southern states have broken away from the American republic and now a battle ensues. While the troop movements on both sides of the Potomac are unknown to each other, through Rose O'Neal Greenhow, *aka Wild Rose or Rebel Rose,* the Confederate Army will know the Union Army's composition and strength and will win the first battle of the War of Northern Aggression, the Battle of First Manassas.

The intelligence network first set up by Governor Letcher is finally going to pay off. Thomas Jordan, *cover name of Thomas John Rayford,* had taught Greenhow a twenty-six symbol cipher to use when transmitting intelligence reports to him *(Figure 4).*

Chapter 2 Trust Bearer

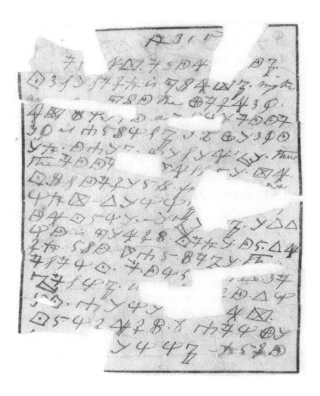

Figure 4. Greenhow Cipher Letter. Courtesy of the National Archives.

Wild Rose observed troop movements within Washington moving toward the Virginia line. Recording and ciphering her findings, she passed them along to her former handler in Virginia, Thomas Jordan. Jordan, no longer serving strictly in a capacity as intelligence collector, had recently been commissioned a lieutenant colonel in the Virginia Provisional Army, becoming General P.T. Beauregard's adjutant.

Outgoing ciphers to Confederate forces in Manassas, Virginia were not passed by Greenhow herself but through one of her couriers she had in her network. This courier that passed on vital intelligence was the young and vivacious Ms. Betty Duvall of Washington City. Upon receiving the message from Wild Rose on 10 July, 1861, Duvall disguised herself as a farm maid and crossed the Potomac River into Virginia via the Chain Bridge. Once she was across, she met up with friends at a known safe house and changed clothes again to make the ride to Fairfax Courthouse, Virginia, where she was to hand off the message. There she met the officer in charge, Confederate General M.L. Bonham. He would later write,

"Upon my announcing that I would have it faithfully forwarded at once, she took out her tucking comb and let fall the longest and most beautiful roll of hair I have ever seen. She took then from the back of her head, where it had been safely tied, a small package, not larger than a silver dollar, sewed up in silk."[29]

This account of how Rose O'Neal Greenhow used her courier to send a message to Confederate forces to prepare them for the Union army is still argued by historians. Many assert that the account and actions that took place were embellished to give Mrs. Greenhow a most "star" status than she really deserved. The only counter to that is that the message she had prepared and had Betty Duvall smuggle across the enemy's lines of advance, in her hair mind you, was later found by Union forces and used to implicate Greenhow, as well as message traffic from ranking Confederate officials thanking her for her assistance.

---

[29] "Intelligence in the Civil War".

On 16 July, 1861, a Union Department of Interior clerk by the name of George Donnellon arrived unannounced to Mrs. Greenhow's home. Rose was a bit skeptical of why this gentleman was at her home, when he handed her a note from Thomas Jordan that read simply, *"Trust Bearer."* Wild Rose wrote out a ciphered message for Donnellon to give to Thomas Jordan. Once the message was received and deciphered by Lt Col Jordan, he passed on the vital intelligence to General P.T. Beauregard. The message read, *"Order issued for McDowell to march on Manassas tonight."* [30] Greenhow wrote down just how she remembered it all occurring:

"On the morning of the 16th of July, the Government papers at Washington announced that the 'grand army' was in motion, and I learned from a reliable source, (having received a copy of the order to McDowell, which could have come from Senator Henry Wilson?), that the order for a forward movement had gone forth...At twelve o'clock on the morning of the 16th of July, I dispatched (sic) a messenger to Manassas, who arrived there at eight o'clock that night. The answer received by me at mid-day on the 17th will tell the purport of my communication –

'Yours was received at eight o'clock at night. Let them come: we are ready for them. We rely upon you for precise information. Be particular as to description and destination of forces, quantity of artillery, &c.

(Signed) THOS. JORDON, Adjt.-Gen.'

---

[30] Merton T. Akers, "Confederate Spy Found Dead", *Reading Eagle*, 26 September 1964.

Chapter 2 Trust Bearer

On the 17th I dispatched (sic) another missive to Manassas, for I had learned of the intention of the enemy to cut the Winchester railroad, so as to intercept Johnson, and prevent his reinforcing Beauregard, who had comparatively but a small force under his command at Manassas(sic).

On the night of the 18th, news of a great victory by the Federal troops at Bull Run reached Washington. Throughout the length and breadth of the city it was cried. I heard it in New York on Saturday, 20th, where I had gone for the purpose of embarking a member of my family for California, on the steamer of the 22nd. The accounts were received with frantic rejoicings, and bets were freely taken in support of Mr. Seward's wise saws - that the rebellion would be crushed out in thirty days. My heart told me that the triumph was premature. Yet, O my God! How miserable I was for the fate of my beloved country, which hung trembling in the balance!
My presentiments were more than justified by the result. On Sunday (21st) the great battle of Manassas was fought, memorable in history as that of Culloden or Waterloo, which ended in the total defeat and rout of the entire 'Grand Army.'...

On the afternoon of that day I left New York for Washington, where I arrived at six o'clock in the morning of the 23rd, in a most impatient mood. Even at that early hour friends were awaiting my arrival, anxious to recount the particulars of the glorious victory. A dispatch (sic) was also received from Manassas by me –

'Our President and our General direct me to thank you. We rely upon you for further information. The Confederacy owes you a debt.

(Signed) THOS. JORDON, Adjt.-Gen.'

My first impulse was to throw myself upon my knees and offer up my tearful thanks to the Father of Mercy for his signal protection in our hour of peril."[31]

The Confederate Army was in debt to Wild Rose and her couriers that had obtained information and passed it on to their forces which won the first battle of many yet to come. Her story does not end there. She would later be arrested in a sting operation by the notorious Pinkerton, imprisoned, travel to Europe on behalf of the Confederate government to sway support, write her memoirs on her exploits, *"My Imprisonment and the First Year of Abolition Rule at Washington"* (which would become a best seller in Europe) before returning home to the Confederate States of America.

The woman that had helped organize the DC spy ring of the Virginia Society that gave birth to the Special and Detached Service and Signal Corps as well as the Richmond Line, died a tragic death at sea. On 1 October, 1864 while attempting to return to her country, the blockade runner she was aboard, the *Condor*, ran aground near the mouth of the Cape Fear River outside of Wilmington while being pursued by the *USS Niphon*. Eager to get ashore, she convinced the captain to allow her to be taken by rowboat. Tragically the rowboat overturned and down with it went Rose O'Neal Greenhow along with Confederate dispatches from Europe and royalties from her memoirs.

---

[31] "Rose O'Neal Greenhow - Confederate Spy," accessed August 14, 2014,
http://www.ourarchives.wikispaces.net/Rose+O%27Neal+Greenhow+-+Confederate+Spy.

Her body was later discovered by a Confederate soldier on the shore. He took the gold that she had with her and pushed her body back into the sea. When again her body was discovered and identified, the soldier felt guilty and returned the gold and apologized stating, "That no respecting Confederate could steal from Mrs. Greenhow". She was buried with full military honors in Wilmington, NC draped in her beloved Confederacy's flag.[32]

The *Wilmington Sentinel* ended the article on the news of her death as:

"At the last day, when the martyrs who have with their blood sealed their devotion to liberty shall stand together firm witnesses that truth is stronger than death, foremost among the shinning throng, coequal with the Rolands and Joan d'Arcs of history will appear the Confederate heroine, Rose A. Greenhow."[33]

"A magician is an actor playing the part of a magician."
– Robert Houdini

The arrest and confinement of Greenhow left an intelligence vacuum which had to be filled. And Letcher, Jordan and Greenhow were no longer in the picture. The man who was chosen to head the spy ring was Benjamin Franklin Stringfellow (1816-1891): *The Master of Disguise*. When one imagines a Southern military hero, arrayed in military garb,

---

[32] Merton T. Akers, "Confederate Spy Found Dead", *Reading Eagle*, 26 September 1964.

[33] "Greenhow Obituary," Wilmington Sentinel, 1 October 1864.

Stringfellow does not come to mind. Though he was a man of short stature, weighing only ninety-four pounds, suffering from a persistent cough, he was able to use these traits to his advantage; qualities others may view as a hindrance.

Earlier he had left his home in Mississippi in hopes of enlisting for the Confederate cause. Being denied on four occasions, he was finally able to join the fifth unit, the Powhatan Troop, later redesignated Company E, 4th Virginia Calvary. Stringfellow (*right*) accomplished this by capturing sentries on guard and marching them to their commander, whom he promised Yankees next time. As one can readily observe, Stringfellow made good use of his being underrated. On  numerous occasions in this manner, he thoroughly outwitted people. So impressive was Stringfellow that he caught the attention of his commanding officer J.E.B. Stuart, who made him his personal scout.

To begin with, he was working in Alexandria and Washington on orders from General Stuart (*I think it was actually coming from Norris since it was early on and the SSB was starting to take shape*). Stringfellow's purpose was intelligence collection along with Edward (E.) Pliny Bryan (*who was a Special and Detached Service and Signal Corps operator*). As it was, he chose to work as a dental assistant for Doctor Richard M. Sykes, a Confederate sympathizer, and went by the cover name of Edward Delcher. Funny thing is, Edward Delcher was a real person and at that time a dentist assistant. In order to make his false persona more convincing, he had Delcher's baptismal paperwork and medical paperwork indicating he was unfit for duty, and a black book that held the most intimate details of the family to whom he now belonged. Stringfellow was able to get all of this documentation because Delcher was from Maryland and Pliny Bryan was friends with his family. In this way, Stringfellow was able to get viable documentation in case anyone was to question his validity.

He even went as far as to wear one of Edward Delcher's "true" suits, complete with a Baltimore tailor tag in it. While working as an assistant, Stringfellow was assisting Bryan in setting up a room in Washington City that had a view over the Potomac so that he could view and relay Confederate signals. The two worked out well together. Stringfellow would become the primary intelligence collector, because when people are nervous they talk; and more so with the dentist or assistant. Bryan would send the message traffic across the river to Confederate sympathizers or other stations, so that it could be deciphered and relayed to Richmond, etc. This, combined with the Doctor Line that had already been established, was morphing into the Richmond Line that would become pivotal in the very near future.[34]

---

[34] Bakeless, 99.

The best thing about his entire cover is that the real Edward Delcher was serving as a Confederate soldier down in Mississippi.[35] Early on Stringfellow discovered that some of the best intelligence to be gathered was in and around the hotel lobbies of the nation's capital; so much that he became a frequent loiterer of such establishments, and sent vital intelligence gathered in these lobbies directly to President Jefferson Davis.[36]

Stringfellow, *The Master of Disguise,* as the title implies, did more than impersonate people of his gender. Upon hearing that his mother had been wounded after Union soldiers occupied her house, he wanted to visit her to see how she was getting along. Also, one of General Stuart's staff officers had just written a book about General Stonewall Jackson, and Stringfellow had him sign it as a present to his mother. As he made his way to her house, he came upon the encampment of Union General Samuel Carter. As a true intelligence agent for the Confederacy, the Master of Disguise made his way into the camp snooping around. He located a captain's uniform and donned it still making his rounds amongst the enemy soldiers gathering intelligence.

Once he reached the tent of the general, he made his way inside and gathered up papers on the general's desk and began to walk out when he was spotted by Union soldiers. He ran for his life being shot at and dropping the book he had brought for his mother. Upon reaching his mother's home, he made

---

[35] Wilson, 64.

[36] Arnold Pavlovsky, *Riding in Circles J.e.b. Stuart and the Confederate Cavalry 1861-1862*, 718.

contact with a family slave who provided him women's clothing to sneak him into the house. He had finally made it and was visiting with his mother when a Union doctor interrupted the visit and Stringfellow hid in the closet. The doctor was there to check up on her injured foot, as he was leaving he gave her the book that was found in the Union camp and informed her that her son was shot dead. The mother of the "dead" Confederate wept as her "dead" son wrote information on the walls of the closet in a true intelligence gathering fashion. He visited with his mother for days and was so convincing that a Union officer commented on how "one frail and wounded woman could eat so much."[37]

Again Stringfellow was to impersonate a female. Sallie Marsden had gone across enemy lines to look for one of her lost brothers and met a Union captain. As fate would have it, the captain was captured by Stringfellow's unit and he had a pass for Sallie on his person hoping she would use it to attend a formal ball with him. The captain asked if Stringfellow would be willing to take a letter to Sallie from him, which he was more than willing to because he had a plan. He delivered the letter to Ms. Sallie and while there acquired clothing needed for a formal ball that a female would wear; and was instructed in proper etiquette by Sallie and her mother.

Stringfellow attended the ball as "Sallie", and while there collected information that General Grant was being moved to command forces against General Lee by the loose tongue of a Union major. The fact that "she" attended the ball without an escort aroused suspicion so much that Stringfellow was

---

[37] Pavlovsky, 67.

escorted home by a Union lieutenant. During the ride, Stringfellow unveiled pistols he had hidden in his dress and instructed the officer to drive to Confederate lines where he had him turned over as a prisoner.[38]

Stringfellow would continue supplying information via his network he had created and perfected. He was even entrusted in March 1865 to present a foreign dignitary with the Confederate terms of surrender to President Lincoln. While awaiting a reply in Washington, he was found collecting intelligence and arrested by Union soldiers, but managed to escape back to the Confederacy.[39] His escape made possible by his source (*auxiliary*) of the Secret Service Bureau which provided him with a horse, carriage, and driver. Possibly provided by Pumphrey who owned a livery that supplied Booth with his horse? However, later in the war, there is an assumption that Stringfellow was involved in the Lincoln assassination because of his connection to certain forms of communication and plans. Later, he also used the Richmond Line to smuggle himself and fiancé across Union lines to Canada to hide out during the conspirator trials. He ended up becoming an Episcopal priest and died in 1913.

The end of his tenure in Washington City doesn't add up. There was already a Confederate peace delegation that had met with Lincoln with no terms agreed upon. Why would there be a single letter sent through a foreign dignitary that possessed terms of surrender? Not only that, but why from Stringfellow?

---

[38] Pavlovsky, 68-69.

[39] Donald E. Markle, *Spies and Spymasters of the Civil War*, (New York: Hippocrene Books, 1994), 113.

This man was very intelligent and crafty, and there was more to him. There is speculation that he was someway involved in the plot to assassinate President Lincoln; mainly because he used the Richmond Line to make his way to Canada. Canada was not a place for your everyday simple intelligence agent of the Confederacy, but your "go-to-guys", as well as the usage of the Richmond Line.

Another piece of incriminating evidence is that he did pass through and stay the night at the home of Mrs. Mary Surratt.[40] Some still argue that there is not enough evidence to implicate Benjamin Franklin Stringfellow for being a conspirator, even though there appears to be just that, as previously mentioned and noted historically.

"Beauty is power; a smile is its sword."
– John Ray

Having been born in Virginia, Isabella Marie Boyd (*left*), like her father who joined the 2nd Virginia Infantry, was a staunch Confederate supporter. As soon as her dad left for the war she resided with her mother in Martinsburg, VA. Her story would begin on 3 July, 1861, when the city was taken by Federal troops. On the following day, Independence Day, it was noticed that the Boyd house was the only house not flying the Stars and Stripes. A Union soldier proceeded to the home and confronted Boyd and her

---

[40] Bakeless, 122.

mother cursing her. Outraged, Boyd pulled out a pistol and killed the soldier at point blank range for insulting her mother. She was acquitted of any wrongdoing but guards were placed around the home.[41] Her nickname was an oxymoron because it was belle, which translates to beautiful in French and Boyd was far from that. She was not known for her attractive face, but her *"good body and best looking ankles".*[42]

Belle Boyd (1843-1900) began to collect intelligence for the Confederate Secret Service Bureau as did many others in her immediate family. She was able to pass freely through Union lines, and on one occasion was able to collect vital intelligence, running through a hail of gun fire and with clothes full of bullet holes, but unscathed. This information, which almost came at the cost her life, has been attributed to why General Stonewall Jackson won the Battle of Front Royal. She was arrested at the age of nineteen for being suspected of being a Confederate agent. While in prison she sang her heart out belting Dixie with all her might to the annoyance of her guards. She was exchanged in December of 1863 and sent to Richmond. The next chapter in her life was to head to England; when she attempted this, her ship was seized by the Union Navy and she was arrested and was on her way back to the United States when destiny struck.[43]

---

[41] "Belle Boyd", accessed August 14, 2014, http://www.nps.gov/resources/person.htm?id=47.

[42] Markle, 156.

[43] Ibid, 156-157.

The commanding officer of the Union ship was Lieutenant S. Wylde Harding, and he and Boyd fell madly in love. She was able to convince him to smuggle her to Canada so she could make it to England, which he was more than willing to do. And while Belle made it to England, Harding was arrested and put in prison for assisting a known Confederate spy. While in England, Belle Boyd was, well, the belle of the ball, no pun intended. Becoming a famous stage actress, Boyd wrote a book on her tales of being a spy and spending time in prison. It became the national best seller in England. Finally in August of 1864, Harding was able to make it to England where he married his beloved Belle. Shortly thereafter, she convinced him to return to the Confederate States of America and work as a "spy." Harding figured it was a good idea as well, and left for the Confederacy, never to see his beloved Belle again. He was captured again, this time as a "rebel spy" and was sent to a Union prison where he died.[44] Belle would eventually make it back to America and on 11 June, 1900, she died and was buried in Wisconsin Dells, WI.[45]

"Mediocrity knows nothing higher than itself but talent instantly recognizes genius."
– Sir Arthur Conan Doyle

The Special and Detached Service and Signal Corps has its own tale of how the signal stations used by the Confederacy, successfully till the end of

---

[44] Markle, 157-158.

[45] "Belle Boyd", accessed August 14, 2014, http://www.nps.gov/resources/person.htm?id=47.

the conflict, came to be and were an annoyance for the Union. Strangely enough, there are historical related books and text that list the Confederacy's signal corps as "primitive" and not as advanced as the Union's which was well established in 1860. Yet, the Union was unable to actually stop the Confederacy from enacting their codes and signals and breaking them. Interesting how this "primitive" organization was able to outsmart the apparently well versed and intellectual Union operatives.

As noted in the first chapter, the separation between the different organizations is complicated at best. However, for this topic of discussion, the Signal Corps was authorized 27 September, 1862 by an act of the Confederate Congress, and by July 1863 Captain William N. Barker was listed as its senior man.

Now why is the Special and Detached Service (SDS) honestly combined with the Signal Corps? Reasoning behind this is the Signal Corps provided the "light" for the blockade runners; and the SDS was organized under the Confederate Department of the Navy, which in all honesty, was comprised of blockade runners who were part of the Secret Navy network. However, because they operated independently of the Confederate Navy, even though the ships were built through questionable means from a Union point of view, they still operated in and out of the ports and stations manned by the Signal Corps. In addition, the cryptic messages from both parties were sent via the Signal Corps through Confederate lines to Richmond, not by the Secret Navy alone. This is why it makes logical sense to include the SDS with the Signal Corps and not with the Secret Navy.

Barker had a great deal on his plate as the commanding officer of the SDS and Signal Corps. For one, he had to ensure that the stations were constantly running, that both friendly and enemy messages were being properly decoded prior to dissemination, that the ports were actively conducting operations to ensure success for the blockade runners as they made their way from European or Caribbean ports. And lastly, that enemy disposition, composition and strength was continually addressed through ciphered messages. The main stations he concerned himself with were Richmond, where he was stationed, Wilmington, NC and Charleston, SC *(Figure 5)*.

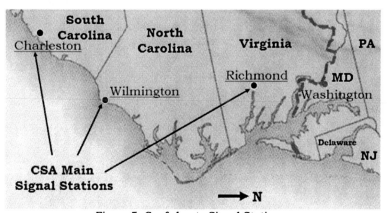

Figure 5. Confederate Signal Stations.

An awkward incident occurred with no real explanation and it involved the commander of the Wilmington station who used to be the executive officer for Norris in Richmond. He was mysteriously sent to Wilmington to command the post there, which allowed Barker to step up and fill the void left by him. This Confederate soldier that was sent to

Wilmington was Lieutenant James Carey. Carey would have been in charge, but for some unexplained reason he was given orders to Wilmington. The commander of the Charleston station was Frank Markoe Jr. Under his command of seventy-six Confederates, he managed to send out information even while under a Union Navy siege.[46]

An issue for Confederate signal men was the laborious time consuming process of encoding and de-ciphering messages. Innovatively, Captain Barker while making life "easier" for his men, implemented the use of an encryption cipher (below).

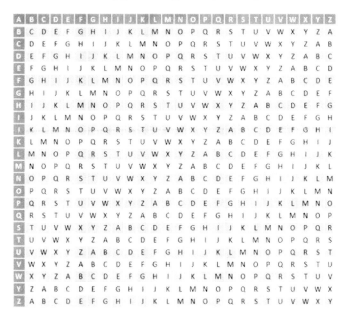

---

[46] J. William Jones, "The Signal Corps in the Confederate States Army," Southern Historical Society Papers, Volume 16, Accessed January 30, 20014
http://www.perseus.tufts.edu/hopper/text?doc=Perseus:text:2001.05.02 73:chapter=1.11.

The *Vigenére Cipher* (which is a polyalphabetic substitution sequence) was used by the Confederacy Signal Corps to encrypt their messages and became time consuming. It was an effective means to communicate because the receiver and sender both had to know the keyword or phrase. Provided is a *Vigenére Cipher with a* message so the complexity can be seen that these men dealt with.

For this example the keyword is: **Trust Bearer.**

The message is: **NAGV AZPF JNV.**

The receiver would write down the message and then the keyword right above it repeating the keyword if necessary. The first letter in the key is 'T,' and the letter under it is 'N.' Take 'T' in the top horizontal column and run down the 'T' vertical column until it intersects the 'N' horizontal column. The letter at the intersection is 'G.' This is substituted in the message for 'G' in Grant. The other letters are converted in the same way, and the message will read:

GRANT AT FARM

This may seem like an easy code to break but the keyword must be known. The Confederacy used only three keywords during the war: MANCHESTER BLUFF, COMPLETE VICTORY and COME RETRIBUTION. As it can be viewed above, this could become a very complicated process. The following is an excerpt from the *Southern Historical Society Papers, Volume 16. By Reverend J. William Jones, Ed.*

On how innovative Barker was, and how he changed the cryptic world:

"To decipher the message, the key was written over it, and the process by which it was put into cipher reversed. To facilitate reading the cipher messages, Captain Wm. N. Barker, of the Signal Corps, invented a simple but convenient apparatus. The alphabetical square was pasted on a cylinder and revolved under a bar, on which was a sliding pointer. Under the pointer and along the bar was pasted the alphabet in a horizontal line. The pointer was brought to the letter in the key on the bar, and the letter in the word to be converted was rolled up under the bar and the pointer rested on the required substitute letter."[47]

Figure 6. A Cipher Disc designed by Francis LaBarre; SS for "Secret Service."

---

[47] J. William Jones, "The Signal Corps in the Confederate States Army," Southern Historical Society Papers, Volume 16, accessed January 30, 2014, http://www.perseus.tufts.edu/hopper/text?doc=Perseus%3Atext%3A20 01.05.0273%3Achapter%3D1.11.

This new invention saved time for the Confederates concerning their ciphered message traffic; and altered the way that messages were decoded and encoded. However, it was to change again when Francis LaBarre of Richmond, VA designed a cipher disc *(Figure 6)*. There are five original discs remaining in the world today.

> *"Inconceivable... You keep using that word. I do not think it means what you think it means."*
> – Inigo Montoya, the Princess Bride

In addition to smuggling arms and supplies into the Confederacy from European ports of call, the blockade runners served as a means to deliver covert messages. Two of the most famous of these "privateers" were Commander John Newland Maffitt of the *Lillian, Florida,* and *Owl* and Lieutenant John Wilkinson of the *Giraffe* and *Chameleon*. Commander Maffitt was known as the *"Prince of the Privateers"* due to his amazing exploits, but was really never a true "privateer" because he was actually a commissioned sailor in the Confederate Navy.

Numerous accounts of how both men miraculously escaped Union blockade vessels abound. Lt. Wilkinson was more than the captain of a blockade runner, he was also an innovator. He designed and implemented the lighting system that was used by the Signal Corps to bring in the ships once they were looking for the shore. One has to remember that the Confederate forts did their best to limit the amount of light they projected as to not silhouette themselves or the Confederate blockade runners. Therefore, once they received the correct signal from an inbound vessel, they would light the way "home" for them; at least when they could. There were at times when this was not feasible and the blockade runners would run their ships aground.

On January 1865, Fort Fisher had fallen to Union forces. Maffitt, aboard the *Owl*, and Wilkinson on the *Chameleon* along with four other ships, were waiting in Bermuda to deliver some much needed supplies to the Confederate Army. Receiving erroneous news that Fort Fisher had repelled the Union invasion, and eager to replenish Lee's Army of Northern Virginia, the small flotilla set sail for Wilmington, NC. Soon after, the Union Navy received a dispatch alerting them of the blockade runners approach, not knowing that Fort Fisher had actually fallen. A plan was devised to make the Confederate ships believe that Fort Fisher was still under Confederate hands by displaying lighting schemes that were typically observed by the ships. To aid in the rouse, all Union ships were ordered to extinguish any lighting they had. The wait was on. The *Owl* was the first to arrive, and upon seeing no lights but only more fires than usual on the embankment, Maffit and the crew became weary of the whole situation. The crew observed a rather large amount of Union ships anchored in water and realized that the fort had fallen. With no choice, they were forced to go back to Bermuda.

Wilkinson aboard the *Chameleon* was spotted not too long after she left port for Wilmington. The crew did everything they could to outrun the chasing Union vessel, the *USS Vanderbilt*, the fastest ship in the blocking fleet. Just as they were beginning to pull away, their engine overheated and was being doused with ocean water to cool it down; allowing the

Vanderbilt to draw closer. After a short time, and to the delight of the crew, the ship's engineer decided that the engines were able to be run again. Now, at full steam and under a full sail, the *Chameleon* pulled away from her pursuer. Lt. Wilkinson made another effort under hours of limited visibility to make good with his cargo to the men of the Confederacy that desperately required it; but a low tide kept him from making good on his endeavor. The Chameleon made way back to Nassau never to run the Union blockades again.[48]

It's always difficult to admit that the losing side of any conflict helped change a certain area or aspect of warfare; because the winning side always wants to lay claim. This was the "start" of the Confederate Special and Detached Service and Signal Corps, by men who were ahead of their time, but rarely received credit for the innovations they created. As noted, the Confederate Signal Corps and Secret Service Bureau was an intelligence and espionage service that was technically and tactically born of its time albeit born before its time. Laying the foundation for special maritime operations, the SDS and Signal Corps detachment's far-reaching influence can readily be felt even today.

---

[48] John F. Blair, *Gray Phantoms of the Cape Fear: Running the Civil War Blockade,* (Winston-Salem, NC: John F. Blair, 1998), 199-202.

Chapter 3
Lost Raiders

"They don't know what they've got there."
– Indiana Jones

Everyone who has read, or in some way or fashion, viewed anything about the Confederate Rangers, instantly think of John S. Mosby and his partisan Rangers. He is inarguably the most famous cavalry leader of the war period; and his dashing looks and his cavalier like persona make him seem as though he was the *Errol Flynn* of the war. Now let's look closely at why these *Rangers* are often called *guerrillas*. Mosby's Rangers could be viewed in the same manner as Roger's Rangers of the French and Indian War and also as the predecessors to the modern day United States Army Special Operation Forces (USASOF).

The Rangers served a **legitimate government body**, and were not a disorganized band of commoners or rebels attempting to cause havoc throughout a region. If Mosby's Rangers are labeled as ever conducting guerilla warfare or utilizing those tactics, then this would imply that they were an illegitimate force, which is not true. However, guerilla warfare is a form of irregular warfare; but then again one is based on the government that created the group's validity.

Therefore, in regards to Mosby's Rangers, they were formed as a quayside militia group by the Confederate States of America, and were a legitimate fighting force. In other words, as soon as Mosby, or any other Confederate Ranger unit, is labeled as conducting guerilla warfare, they are considered illegitimate as well as the government they fall under. This, however, is not true, due to the fact that the Confederacy, operating with three systems of a republican form of government, coining currency, possessing a military fighting force, with diplomatic relations with other world powers, and having their own commerce system, is therefore considered a legitimate government.

Once the Union labeled them *guerillas*, it affected their reputability throughout the world, and meant that every single action these *Rangers* conducted was *illegal* and *immoral*. Why is this so? Easy, President Lincoln wanted to delegitimize the government. He wanted the Confederacy viewed as rebels that broke away in order to overthrow the Union, rather than as a party that broke away from another country to form a more perfect union in their own eyes. Definitions that are attached to people, units, or detachments have underlying meanings that many people tend not to think about, and unwittingly perpetuate. The operations conducted by the Confederate Rangers can be labeled, pure and simple, as unconventional warfare.

Confederate Rangers could also be viewed as **paramilitary forces,** *because they were a force(s) or group(s) distinct from the regular armed forces of any country, but resembling them in organization, equipment, training, or mission.* [49] The Confederate Rangers of the Civil War conducted many raids, which was often their most common form of offensive action. Now there are phases and elements of a raid. Importantly, we need to discuss the purpose for

---

[49] Department of the Army, *FM 1-02 (FM 101-5-1) Operational Terms and Graphics*, 1-142.

them. There are **three (3) basic purposes of a raid**: *1) to gain access to a facility or specific location, 2) the inability to secure a site, and by that showing the lack in security of a (critical) facility, and 3) to acquire goods or materiel.* This leads into what a **seizure** is in regards to military terms; a seizure *involves the capture of a building, object, or complex that has or contains any value of the labeled enemy.* The Rangers were also extremely skilled in conducting **hasty attacks**, where *planning and time for an operation is substituted for speed and surprise to exploit an opportunity.*

There could also be a debate that the various Ranger detachments were an unorganized group or even vigilantes that were just moving throughout occupied or enemy territories killing at will. This brings us to the term of **vigilante**; a *group that organizes without government authority to enforce its own concept of laws and order.*[50] The only reasoning for conducting such actions is for personal self-interests. However, from the beginning of the conflict the Rangers were far from vigilantes. In fact, they were given government authority to conduct their actions. Besides, they too used restraint. For example, an established fact was Mosby prohibited his men from looting, pillaging, and engaging in summary executions. On 5 June, 1862, *The Daily Dispatch* in Richmond, VA wrote about this topic due

---

[50] Department of the Army, *FM 1-02 (FM 101-5-1) Operational Terms and Graphics*, 1-155.

-If more information is desired to better understand the true essence of a military style raid and the mechanics involved, a great additional reference would be US Army Special Forces Small Unit Tactics by Paul LeFavor.

to controversy surrounding the various Confederate Ranger detachments:

It is thought by some — and that belief operates to the prejudice of enlistments in these corps — that Partisan Rangers are nothing more or less than guerillas, roving parties, independent of all authority and law, and as such are not entitled to the protection of the code of civilized warfare. On the contrary an act of Congress has established this branch of the service, of which the officers are regularly commissioned by the President. The men are paid and provided as in the regular service, with the addition of receiving the value of the arms and munitions of war which they may capture from the enemy. They are designed to operate beyond the lines of our armies. That they will be in constant conflict with the enemy is most likely, and that the warfare they carry on may be very bloody; but it does not follow if they, on their part, observe the rules of civilized warfare, that they will not receive them in turn.

If the enemy shall attempt to deprive our partisan warriors of those advantages which other prisoners are guaranteed by the civilized code, not only may the partisans themselves retaliate upon the enemy, but President Davis himself would doubts feel called upon to in later pose for their protection Let no one, then, be deterred from enlisting with the partisans under the apprehension that they will be treated as brigands or pirates. They stand upon as high a ground, nay, upon the same ground, as do the regular and provisional armies.[51]

The Confederate Congress approved the **1862 Partisan Rangers Act** to allow more Southern men

---

[51] Cowardin & Hammersley, "The Daily Dispatch: June 5, 1862," *Southern Historical Society Papers*, accessed January 30, 2014, http://www.perseus.tufts.edu/hopper/text?doc=Perseus%3Atext%3A20 06.05.0493.

to join the ranks of the Confederate fighting force without having to actually raise their hand to join.[52] The point being made here is that these men were granted their positions via a **mandate**. This is because they *were given a commission, authorization, and charter of authority within the Confederate War Department to carry out specific responsibilities*. Now their responsibilities may have differed from hour to hour or day to day, but they were given a job to do and granted the power to take necessary action(s) to achieve the overall ends state from the individual that granted the mandate.

Little is spoken of or written about the other Confederate Ranger groups out there on the battlefield that existed. There is much written on Mosby and his Rangers, and rightfully so, since he contributed a great deal of information to the Secret Service Bureau, and was possibly even the best "on the ground" intelligence gatherer that the Confederate States of America possessed. He and his men were not the only ones out there providing information or conducting other actions. [53] These *"others"* who contributed greatly to the war effort included; the Iron Scouts, Reid's Rangers, Terry's Texas Rangers, Cobb's Scouts, Johnson's Spy Company, and the Navarro Spies. Looking at some of the names of these detachments, the word *spy* or *spies* is used, and it had a different meaning in the 19th century and was used synonymously with the

---

[52] Kathy Still, "Partisan Rangers Act had unintended consequences, Civil War expert contends," last modified September 26, 2014, http://www.uvawise.edu/News/Partisan-Rangers-Act-had-unintended-consequences-Civil-War-expert-contends.

[53] "Intelligence in the Civil War".

word *Rangers*. Here is a clear example of the word usage,

> *"The object of the plan is to keep twenty or thirty mounted men continually on the frontier as* **spies** *(Rangers); as well for the preventing of incursions or small parties of Indians..."*[54]

This was a plan by the *Impresario* Stephen F. Austin, on 28 August 1826 concerning the Rangers which were the militia of the colony of Coahuila y Tejas (Texas); a clear example of the word spy or spies being a synonym for Ranger.

> *"Some folks look at me and see a certain swagger,*
> *which in Texas is called 'walking."*
> *– George W. Bush*

When Texas Rangers are thought of, people often think Chuck Norris or the Walker Revolver, but there were others out there and they played a role in the Confederate Intelligence network. One such Ranger was a man named Benjamin McCulloch *(left)*. He was feared by the Union once it was announced that the Mexican War and frontier Ranger hero had raised a group of 500 Texas

---

[54] Allen G. Hatley, *Early Texas Indian Wars, 1822-1835* (Honolulu, HI: Talei Publications, 2005), 109.

Rangers to fight for the Confederacy. There was
hysteria up and down the eastern seaboard, which
reached as far as Washington and New York. The
people feared that he was going to apprehend or kill
President Lincoln and then seat himself at the seat of
power of the United States government, and there
would be no one to stop him. He would ultimately
rule the nation.[55] All of this occurred because word
was leaked that he had raised a company of Rangers
to serve the Confederacy. The American people feared
the Rangers because of their war-fighting prowess.
The following tale elaborates the exploits of Ranger
McCulloch:

*"On the second day out and on the head waters of Peach
creek, they struck a fresh trail of foot Indians, bearing
directly for Gonzales. This, of course, changed their plans.
Duty to their threatened neighbors demanded that they
should follow and break up this invading party. They
followed the trail rapidly for three or four hours and then
came in sight of the enemy, who promptly entered an
almost impenetrable thicket bordering a branch and in a
post oak country. The hostiles, concealed from view, had
every advantage, and every attempt to reach a point from
which they could be seen or fired upon was exposing the
party attempting it to the fire of the unseen enemy. Several
hours passed in which occasional shots were fired.*

*From the first Capt. Jim refused to enter or allow his men
to enter the thicket, saying the danger was too great and
Toncahuas too scarce to run such hazards. One of his men,
however, from behind the only tree well situated for
defense, was killed, the only loss sustained by the
attacking party. Finally, impatient of delay and dreading
the approach of night, McCulloch got a promise from Capt.
Jim to so place his men around the lower end of the thicket*

---

[55] Mike Cox, *The Texas Rangers: Wearing the Cinco Peso, 1821-1900,*
(New York: Forge Books, 2008), 173.

as to kill any who might attempt to escape, while he, his brother, Randall and Henson would crawl through it from the upper end. Wolfin declined a ticket in what he regarded as so dangerous a lottery. Slowly they moved, observing every possible precaution till---"one by one"----each of the four killed an Indian and two or three others were wounded. The assailed Indians fired many shots and arrows, but seemed doomed to failure. In thickets nothing is so effective as the rifle ball.

Finally the survivors of the enemy (nine of an original thirteen) emerged in the branch at the lower end of the thicket and were allowed by Capt. Jim to escape. When the whites effected an exit the enemy was beyond reach, sheltered in a yet larger thicket. This closed the campaign. The Toncahuas, scalping the four dead hostiles, felt impelled by a patriotic sense of duty to hasten home and celebrate their victory. They fleeced off portions of the thighs and breasts of the dead and all started in; but they soon stopped on the way and went through most of the mystic ceremonies attending a war dance, thoroughly commingling weird wails over their fallen comrade with their wild and equally weird exaltations over their fallen foes. This ceremony over, they hastened home to repeat the savage scenes with increased ferocity. McCulloch and party, more leisurely, returned to Gonzales, to be welcomed by the people who had thus been protected from a night attack by the discomfited invaders. Such inroads by foot Indians almost invariably resulted in the loss of numerous horses, and one or more---alas! Sometimes many---lives to the settlers."[56]

McCulloch's actions previously in other engagements gave meaning to the phrase, *Texas Ranger;* and as others would use the phrase that

---

[56] John Henry Brown, "Defeat of Comanches and Wacos on Peach Creek ca. 1838," The Indian Wars and Pioneers of Texas, accessed August 23, 2014,
http://www.tamu.edu/faculty/ccbn/dewitt/indiantales.htm.

would hail from the *Lone Star State*, they too would be held in the same regard, especially when it was known that they had served with Ben McCulloch.

What has to be remembered is that the Texas Rangers had also fought in the Mexican-American War with many of the same officers and men that were now involved in the War of Northern Aggression on both sides. The Texas Rangers of the Texas Revolution had become famous within the Republic of Texas and surrounding territories and States. It wasn't until the Mexican-American War that the Texas Rangers and their exploits were thrust into the American spotlight, and this helped the name "Rangers" during the War of Northern Aggression. Their exploits during the Mexican-American War made them even more famous; and any unit being called Rangers were put in the same category as them. The main characters of these exploits were; Ben McCulloch (no surprise there), John C. Hays, Robert A. Gillespie, and Samuel H. Walker. These four men were the key leaders that kept the Ranger Companies intact for the duration of the war because they were, "influencing people by providing purpose, direction, and motivation while operating to accomplish the mission and improving the organization".[57]

They were extremely skilled at intelligence gathering, and the dissemination of information to the regular American forces under General Zachary Taylor; ensuring victory during the Mexican-America War. Another factor that made the Rangers successful as "spies" or scouts was their drive and determination against the Mexicans for their devilish

---

[57] Department of the Army, *FM 1-02 (FM 101-5-1) Operational Terms and Graphics*.

exploits against Texans at the Alamo, Goliad, Santa Fe, and Mier. This war was also covered by the newspapers that were battling for the best stories so their respective newspaper would sell throughout the Union. The Rangers gave them the stories they needed, and the Rangers got the press they deserved.[58]

> *"All new states are invested, more or less, by a class of noisy, second-rate men who are always in favor of rash and extreme measures. But Texas was absolutely overrun by such men."*
> *– Sam Houston*

One such unit from Texas, that used the word "Rangers" simply to strike fear into the hearts of the Union foe, was *Terry's Texas Rangers.* Therefore, because those men decided to use the word "Rangers" in their name, they were using a **psychological operations approach.** This is a *technique adopted to induce a desired reaction on the part of the target audience.*[59] What is being inferred here is, that they were attempting to drive the same fear into the hearts and minds of their Yankee foe, just as the *Texas Rangers* had done throughout Texas and Mexico during the Mexican-American War. This corps of Rangers were formed by Benjamin F. Terry, Thomas S. Lubbock and John J. Wharton, all of which were actual Texas Rangers themselves, hence the name, and comprised of men that were the

---

[58] Cox, 105-106.

[59] Department of the Army, *FM 1-02 (FM 101-5-1) Operational Terms and Graphics*, 1-153.

roughest Rangers, both current and former, to man the ranks.[60] Lubbock's brother at the time was also the governor of Texas (the city and county known today in the State is named for *Thomas* not his brother).[61]

This group of cavalrymen were raised to join the Army of Northern Virginia, but were rerouted to the Army of the Tennessee under the command of a fellow Texan.[62] The Rangers are not that well known because they weren't used in a propaganda-like manner as Mosby and his Rangers were. Later, re-designated the 8th Texas Calvary by the Confederate War Department, a pejorative to Terry's Rangers (preferring the title "Rangers"), the unit conducted more operations than a normal cavalry unit would ever conduct, as well as protecting the flanks during battle. Further, they were also skilled in the ability to conduct scouting or intelligence gathering operations and did so for General Joseph E. Johnston of the Army of the Tennessee.

These Rangers also conducted *subversion,* not *sabotage,* against the Union supply rail lines that were being used by General William T. Sherman's army on their march through the Southern States.[63]

---

[60] James B. Gillett, *Six Years with the Texas Rangers, 1875 to 1881,* (Lincoln, NE: Bison Books University of Nebraska Press, 1976), 30.

[61] "Terry's Texas Rangers," accessed September 24, 2014, http://www.bbcwr.us/8th_texas_cavalry.html.

[62] Michael J. McAfee, Don Troiani's Regiments and Uniforms of the Civil War (Mechanicsburg, PA: Stackpole Books, 2014), 193.

[63] Thomas W. Cutrer, "EIGHTH TEXAS CAVALRY, TERRY'S TEXAS RANGERS," Handbook of Texas Online. (http://www.tshaonline.org/handbook/online/articles/qke02), accessed

Chapter 3 Lost Raiders

Commenting on one of the numerous actions and raids in support of the Army of the Tennessee, led Regimental Chaplain Robert Franklin Bunting to write on 9 September 1864, while at camp in Florence, AL:

"We see by the Northern papers that the clamor is everywhere for peace. Many demand it on any terms, but peace they must and will have...The goal and prize are not far ahead of us...We have done considerable fighting. When the raid is over I will write you fully."[64]

Terry's Rangers were well versed in conducting reconnaissance missions, as was the primary role of the cavalry units during the war, and collected vital information required by the Confederate government. The information collected was sent via the signal stations, or through various other means that have been described. One such Ranger was Captain Alexander May Shannon of Terry's Rangers. His detachment became known as *"Shannon's Scouts".* They were also tasked with picking off the looting and foraging parties sent out by General Sherman.

Due to the superior intelligence that he and his Rangers were passing up to the Confederate SSB, he was promoted to Colonel and made the officer-in-

May 14, 2014. Uploaded on June 12, 2010. Modified on March 4, 2011. Published by the Texas State Historical Association.

[64]R. Steven Jones, "Our Trust is in the God of Battles: The Civil War Letters of Robert Franklin Bunting, Chaplain, Terry's Texas Rangers, C.S.A.,227," accessed September 15, 2014, http://muse.jhu.edu/journals/swh/summary/v111/111.2.jones.html, 274.

charge of the SSB detachment of the Army of the Tennessee. [65] This meant that all vital intelligence would be passed through him prior to going up to the Confederate War Department and the general officers that required the information for an upcoming plan of action.

Like Shannon's Scouts, there were other imbedded sub-detachments within Terry's Rangers. They were; the Johnson Spy Company, Company E, the Navarro Spies (later Navarro Independent Rifles), and Company F. Captain B.D. McKie was to command the Navarro Spies that were raised in Navarro County, TX. He was renowned, not only for his selfless service and concern for his men's wellbeing, but his daring exploits while collecting information for the Confederate government. In 1863, while conducting his last raid in which his men observed him leading the charge, Captain McKie was shot twice, but refused to leave the saddle, instead electing to stay in the fight with his fellow cavalrymen. The third shot, forcing him from the saddle, necessitated his leaving the field of battle to recover from the wounds he had sustained. However, the Lord Almighty saw it fit to take Captain B.D. McKie, and he succumbed to his wounds, never to see the war again.

Another Ranger leader, Captain Alf Johnson of the Johnson Spy Company, was well known throughout the State of Texas prior to the war. This was due to his exploits with Texas Ranger friend Ben McCulloch. Due to his frequent raiding parties on Federal camps, his detachment was also one of the most hated scouting units during the war. One of the best told stories is that of Johnson escaping Yankee

---

[65] R. Steven Jones, 329.

capture while on a reconnaissance mission. While going into Springfield, MO to collect the composition of General Fremont's army, he and Captain Mabry *(Camp Mabry in Texas is named after his son, not him)* found themselves in quite a predicament.

Terry's Texas Rangers (Courtesy Battle Born Civil War Reenactors).

The two men were discovered and surrounded in a house from which they were conducting surveillance. Knowing that surrender was not an option, Captain Mabry flung open the front door, firing on every Union soldier within proximity, providing cover fire for Captain Johnson; who at the same time threw open a window and jumped out. As soon as his feet hit the ground, he opened up with his double barrel shotgun into the Union soldiers that were attempting to apprehend him.

The two men mounted their steeds and made their

way back to the camp. Upon arrival, their first priority was not themselves, but that the information they had collected was disseminated properly. Captain Johnson was wounded in the leg and Captain Mabry through the hand. Johnson would not live to see the end of the war either, as he died enroute to a Federal Prisoner of War Camp in 1863.[66]

"Carolina! Carolina! Heaven's Blessings Attend Her! While We Live We Will Cherish, Protect And Defend Her."
– North Carolina State Song

Of the Ranger detachments that served the Confederacy, most were strictly in the business of intelligence gathering and foraging. An ability to strike fear into the hearts of the enemy, without even having to be present, was another asset the Rangers possessed. Confederate Rangers were the scourge of the Union armies. One such unit was Spencer's Rangers Independent Calvary of North Carolina. This unit was commanded by Captain William H. Spencer and was comprised of 86 riders when the unit was formed on 7 February 1863. J.W. Evans, a Corporal in the 68th, which at one time, Spencer's Rangers were members of, wrote down in his own words the type of duty this unit was performing.

They did not consider themselves as "guerrillas". The guerrillas were the ones causing havoc on their own people; another clear example of the use of words in the descriptive process. The Union and pro-Union sympathizers viewed them as "guerrillas"

---

[66] Anne Bailey, *Between the Enemy and Texas: Parsons's Texas Cavalry in the Civil War*, (College Station, TX: Texas A&M University Press, 2013), 44-45.

because they thought the Confederacy was attempting to overthrow and undermine the United States government; when in all reality they were just attempting to fight against what they *(the Confederacy)* viewed as an invasion, and an act of war on their own land, their newly formed country. What words are chosen to describe a people will follow them to the ends of the earth. A similar example would be the Revolutionary War, where the Americans were called "rebels" but did not see themselves that way.

These so called "guerrillas" were fighting against and defending against actual local guerrilla forces. This is where the word play and lack of understanding causes confusion and improper labeling. Spencer's Rangers were a group of rangers that collected information within the State of North Carolina and sent that intelligence up the chain-of-command, as well as scouting, foraging, and protecting the property of the citizens of the State. Spencer's Rangers were captured though, while in winter quarters by Union troopers of the First Pennsylvania Volunteers. The report of the capture:

General Orders No. 24.

Hdqrs. Army and Dist. of N. Carolina, New Berne, N. C., March 2, 1864.

The commanding general is gratified at being enabled to announce another in the series of successful enterprises against the enemy projected by Brigadier-General Wessells, commanding Sub-district of the Albemarle. The army gun-boat Foster, Captain McLaughlin commanding, with a

detachment of infantry under Lieutenant Helm, One Hundred and First Pennsylvania Volunteers, was sent on the 16th of February on an expedition to Fairfield N. C., where a band of <u>guerrillas</u> under command of Captain Spencer was quartered. The camp was surprised, the arms and stores secured, and the whole company taken prisoners without loss on our side. The affair was conducted in a severe snow-storm, and reflects much credit upon the officers and men concerned.
By command of Major-General Peck:

Benj. B. Foster, Assistant Adjutant-General.[67]

What is interesting about this communique is that Foster, the Assistant-Adjutant General, list the men captured as guerillas; however Major General John J. Peck did not in his message. It is interesting how the more senior individual did not see the Confederates as guerillas (since they were not) but the junior officer did. Another lesser known "guerrilla" band was the Company of Partisan Rangers, "Hyde's Rangers" under the direct command of Edward S. Swindell. This unit was comprised of 90 rangers and is better known for conducting a raid on 4 March 1863 near Swan Quarter, conflicting substantial damage, while losing five partisan Rangers themselves. There is not much known about this unit other than this raid.

"What does it all mean, Basil?"
– Austin Powers

---

[67] United States War Department, *The War of the Rebellion: A Compilation of the Official Records of the Union and Confederate Armies,* (Washington D.C.: Government Printing Office, 1901), 60.

Chapter 3 Lost Raiders

The men that made up the variety of ranging units within the Confederate War Department were skilled, with or without publication of their daring exploits. No matter where each of these units were, they were all collecting intelligence and sending it "up the chain" hoping it would lead to Confederate victories. They were skilled in the art of **exploitation** which is, *taking full advantage of any information that has come to hand for tactical, operational, or strategic purposes.*[68]

You may be asking yourself, well what does that mean? It means that no matter how minute the information, the Rangers sent it on. The smallest piece may be what was needed. Each agent throughout the Secret Service Bureau was collecting intelligence, but that last piece needed to fill in the puzzle in order to complete the plan may have come from a Ranger. Let's take into account a Mosby and Stuart combined action *(you know Mosby had to be mentioned eventually)*.

In June of 1863, Col. John Singleton Mosby, aka *The Grey Ghost*, was out for the day conducting operations when General J.E.B. Stuart made his way into Middleburg, VA (considered the heart of *"Mosby's Confederacy"*). The location Stuart chose as his headquarters was the *Red Fox Inn,* which was the favorite watering hole and relaxation spot for Mosby and his Rangers. Stuart had intelligence of the Union composition and disposition, but pieces were missing. Mosby had his own intelligence, and when the two combined, what they had enabled them to make a tactically sound decision for an upcoming

---

[68] Department of the Army, *FM 1-02 (FM 101-5-1) Operational Terms and Graphics*, 1-76.

battle.[69] Recall now, the scrawny guy that had a cover as a dentist assistant in Alexandria, VA – Benjamin Franklin Stringfellow.

Stringfellow was initially trained by J.E.B. Stuart and used as an intelligence agent. Therefore, it can be assumed that Stuart (*below*) was working for Major Norris, because Stringfellow was an agent working for the Signal Corps, and the Rangers fell under the SSB as raiders, scouts, and battlefield intelligence gatherers. Stuart said of Stringfellow,  *"In determining the enemy's real design, I rely upon you, as well as the quick transmission of the information."*[70]

The entire network of information and how that information was passed along went full circle; an intertwining web of communication lines which had to be confusing not only for those in command, but also for the operatives in the field, on who they worked for and answered to. It's only fitting now to discuss one of Mosby's dashing victories when hopelessly outnumbered.

On 2 March, 1863, Union troopers of the 18th Pennsylvania Cavalry were given intelligence that Mosby and his Rangers were in the Middleburg area. Therefore, they devised a plan to raid the town, get

---

[69] Get Lost in Loudon, *"Hunting the Grey Ghost,"* YouTube video, accessed June 7, 2013.

[70] "Intelligence in the Civil War".

confirmation on his exact whereabouts and seize him. What the Union soldiers didn't count on was the fact that maybe Mosby and his boys weren't in town. Upon being assured that neither Mosby nor any Rangers were in Middleburg, the Union soldiers freed some slaves, took some older men and children as prisoners, and made their way to Aldie Mill, just down the road from Middleburg. Later that day, Mosby made his way into Middleburg after skirmishing with the 1st Vermont.

The townspeople wasted no time informing Mosby of the insult they recently endured, so Mosby and his men quickly rode towards Aldie Mill. Mosby reached the mill before any of his Rangers, and was actually  a good mile ahead of his men because he had just received a fresh horse (captured from the Union) that was faster than the other horses. The Union soldiers of the 18th Penn saw only Mosby (left) wielding two Colt 44 revolvers charging at them screaming the rebel yell. The Union soldiers dove into the flour bins and took cover. Mosby's recently acquired horse had not yet learned to stop on Mosby's command, and kept going past the mill.

The horse eventually stopped at a bridge and desaddled Mosby, who fell into the mud. Unashamed and determined, Mosby made his way back up to the mill to finish what he had started. By the time the rest of his Rangers had reached the mill, the "Grey Ghost" had captured fifty Union troopers and freed the captive Middleburg citizens on his own; while still covered in mud. Knowing of Mosby's accolades, poet Herman Melville wrote this about Mosby's Confederacy, *"As glides in seas the shark rides Mosby through green dark . . ."* [71]

These Rangers of the Confederacy were not guerrillas in any way shape or form; however, the Union did not agree. On one account, the 36th Ohio was on a scouting mission attempting to locate, what they labeled as "guerrilla" parties in what is now West Virginia. They found a young man casting bullets and determined that was enough to label him as a "guerilla". The Union soldiers bounded the young man and began to march him back to camp. Not too far from where he was taken captive, two of the soldiers fell back with the young man. William Dunham, an officer of the 26th Ohio Regiment recalled what happened next:

"The corporal told the fellow now was his time to escape and for him to run for his life, he did so, not seeming to know the object, when a few paces off the Prices (brothers in the regiment) fired upon him and brought him to the ground, A. Price then ran up and shot him again with the pistol he took from the man...and thus put an end to his life...the boys described his screams after he was shot first as heart-rendering...they left him unburied...My God: has it come to this?" [72]

---

[71] Get Lost in Loudon, "Hunting the Grey Ghost".

[72] Reid Mitchell, *Civil War Soldiers: Their Expectations and Their Experiences,* (New York: Penguin Books, 1988), 135.

Chapter 4
Secret Navy

"I know not all that may be coming, but be it
what it will, I'll go to it laughing."
– Melville, Moby-Dick

The populace of the Confederate States of America, as well as the military, was being strangled by Abraham Lincoln's *"Anaconda Plan"*. This plan was to blockade 3,000 miles of Confederate coastline to keep goods and material from coming in and going out. The *Commission on Conference* headed by Commander Dupont was the first to suggest the institution of this plan to the Union President. The biggest issue they had was how to stop the blockade runners since their naval fleet was too slow. Along came the suggestion of using the U.S. Revenue Cutter Service (predecessor to the United States Coast Guard) to help combat the smaller Confederate ships with their own fast moving vessels. The government of the Confederacy knew that they had to find a way to crack the Federals back by attacking and seizing their goods that were leaving and attempting to come into Northern ports.[73] This action taken by the Union against the Confederacy is why the Confederate Secret Navy was developed and initiated.

The plan devised to combat this blockade and deal with the Federal ships was envisioned by Stephen R. Mallory. Mallory was forty-nine at the time of his appointment as the Secretary of the Confederate

---

[73] US Navy, Civil War Warfare Documentary, YouTube video, accessed June 7, 2013.

Navy. And though his assignment was protested by many within the new capital in Montgomery, Alabama, he was the only real viable choice for President Davis. Mallory had served in the United States Senate with Jefferson, was from the State of Florida, and served as the committee chair of Naval Affairs. Being from Florida meant that it would allow Jefferson to have each of the new States of the Confederate Government represented in his cabinet; however his only downfall was that he was Roman Catholic. This religious preference did not sit well with a very Protestant South; who viewed Catholics as enemies of the State.[74] Being as such, this did not stop President Jefferson Davis from making the appointment. Like John H. Reagan, the appointment of Mallory proved to be one of Jefferson's most exceptional appointments made during his tenure as President. Mallory had to find a man to help him with the task of ridding the Confederacy of that annoying blockade on their territorial waters; and this man would be James Dunwoody Bulloch, the future CSA Navy Chief Agent in Europe. Bulloch was a man that would change how clandestine operations would be conducted and challenged; a transition from clandestine to overt operations.

"It is not that life ashore is distasteful to me. But life at sea is better."
– Sir Francis Drake, Sea Captain

James Dunwoody Bulloch was a Georgia born former sailor in the United States Navy. He would

[74] James Tertuis de Kay, *The Rebel Raiders: The Astonishing History of the Confederacy's Secret Navy,* (New York: The Random House Publishing Group, 2002), 4-5.

later hold the distinction of becoming the uncle of the future President of the United States, Theodore Roosevelt. Bulloch (below) had to figure out how to get the much needed ships built and where. Through much deliberation, it was decided that the ships should be built by Great Britain, a friend, and hopefully so to be, ally of the Confederacy. He had

already secured contracts with some shipbuilding companies in Birkenhead and Liverpool to build at least two *"Secret Navy Ships of the Line"* or ironclad rams. Great Britain was willing to assist the Confederate States because they longed for a divided United States of America, so the country wouldn't become an international powerhouse.[75]

Bulloch played a constant cat and mouse game against the Union operatives that were watching his every move. These Union agents passed information through Charles Francis Adams Sr., the United States Minister (Ambassador) to Great Britain. [76] However, Bulloch had an ingenious way of orchestrating the contracts with the European shipbuilders. When he attended meetings with these builders, Bulloch conducted business as a civilian

---

[75] Emory M. Thomas, *The Confederate Nation: 1861-186,* (New York: First Harper Perennial Edition Published, 2011), 128-129.

[76] de Kay, 66-67.

rather than as a member of the Confederate government. This enabled Bulloch to buy time whenever there was new intelligence collected on his ships. The main issue dealt with specifications. If the Union could prove that a ship was to be used in support of the Confederacy, then they could ensure that the ship in question would never be allowed to sail outside of British territorial waters; and must be apprehended according to British law.

Three of the most famous and dangerous ships to the Union which Bulloch had commissioned were the *Enrica (or 290), Oreto,* and the *Sea King.* These were the cover names for each of these vessels; as each would come to be known respectively as the *Alabama, Florida, and Shenandoah.*[77] Each ship was manufactured under clandestine means, and then once outside of Britain's territorial waters, the battle flag was raised, thus becoming an overt action. Union diplomats in England were trying with all their might, day in and day out, to stop the Laird Yard, which constructed *290* and *Oreto,* from having their keels touch the open waters of the Atlantic Ocean. Union agents, in full swing, had gathered a great deal of intelligence on these two vessels. Time and time again, there were attempts to stop the manufacturing of the vessels citing that each was being built under false pretenses.

All the while, Confederate counterespionage detachments did their part by thwarting Union agents from obtaining vital key intelligence. One such vital piece, collected by Confederate agents was the arrival of the *USS Tuscarora,* no doubt brought in to stop Confederate ships of war from leaving Britain's territorial waters. Bulloch had to devise a

---

[77] "Intelligence in the Civil War", 38-39.

plan on how to get these ships out to the open ocean without drawing any more suspicion.[78] Bulloch was receiving information from a source within Whitehall about actions and dealings that the British government was having with the Union. This source must have been at the highest level, and with great speculation, it can be surmised that it was Lord John Russell, the Foreign Secretary of the British Government.[79]

The *Oreto* or *Florida (below)* left under the guise as a leisure vessel, only to be fitted with a Confederate States crew to wreak havoc on Union shipping.

Figure 4-1. CSS Florida. Courtesy of the National Archives.

The American diplomats in London were determined not to let the *290* or *Enrica* leave the port

---

in Liverpool. Minister Adams had sent a letter of complaint to the British government citing that an earlier interpretation of the law and of the true nature of the *290* was incorrect; and that she was to be seized at once to maintain diplomatic ties with the United States of America.

The letter was given to Lord Russell, and before he had the chance to read his mail, he was interrupted because the Queens Advocate, Sir John Harding, had been struck down with a "seizure". Harding was needed to interpret the claim, as legal or not, to stop the *290*. Not to mention, that all of this is occurring on a Friday and offices were open for only a half day on Saturday. Russell and his undersecretary debated on whether or not they should seek guidance from another office within the government since the Queens Advocate was unable to perform his duties. The entire day was spent debating the issue and the complaint was not passed on. On Saturday, discovering that Sir Harding was still not well, Lord Russell ordered that the letter be sent to the Attorney General, William Atherton, and promptly left for the weekend. The Undersecretary, Austen Layard, had the office clerks compile all the evidence, proofread, and copy it before it was sent on to Atherton's office. By the time the packet of dispute reached Atherton's office he was gone for the weekend to return on Monday. That very same Friday an informant sent Bulloch a letter informing him that the *290* should leave port within 48 hours or she will never be able to leave.[80]

An account of the capture of the *CSS Florida aka Oreto* from a Union Naval Officer follows:

---

[80] de Kay, 63-65.

In the absence of Captain Morris, who was on shore, Lieutenant Thomas K. Porter, formerly of the United States Navy, came on board and surrendered the Florida, with fifty-eight men and twelve officers, making at the same time an oral protest against the capture. Five of the Florida's officers, including her commander, and the remainder of her crew, were on shore. We took a hawser to the Florida and towed her to sea. In contemplating the attack on the Florida in the bay, I thought it probable the Brazilian authorities would forbear to interfere, as they had done at Fernando de Noronha, when the rebel steamer Alabama was permitted to take into the anchorage three American ships, and to take coal from the Louisa Hatch within musket-shot of the fort, and afterward, within easy range of their guns, to set on fire those unarmed vessels. I regret, however, to state that they fired three shotted guns at us while we were towing the Florida out. Fortunately we received no damage. After daylight a Brazilian sloop-of-war, in tow of a paddle gun-boat, was discovered following us. With the aid of sail on both vessels we gradually increased our distance from them. We had three men slightly wounded; one only of the three is now on the sick report.

I enclose a list of the prisoners. Those who have a star opposite their names were formerly in the United States navy. This vessel is ready for service. The Florida will require repairs of machinery, a new mizzen-mast, etc. The officers and crew manifested the best spirit. They have my thanks for their hearty co-operation, in which I beg to include Thomas F. Wilson, Esq., United States Consul at Bahia, who volunteered for any duty.

I am, sir, very respectfully, your obedient servant,
       N. Collins, Commander. [81]

---

[81] James Dunwody Bulloch, *The Secret Service of the Confederate States in Europe* (New York: G.P. Putnam's Sons, 1884), 203.

Chapter 4 Secret Navy

At this point you may be asking: What does this have to do with the Confederate Secret Service Bureau and Signal Corps? Well, a great deal actually. This was about the clandestine operations that the Confederate Navy conducted, while agents of the Secret Service Bureau simultaneously were ensuring the success of those operations. This is where the two agencies, yet both entirely separate, assisted each other in a very beneficial way.

"The game is afoot."
– Sherlock Holmes

The Union did everything in its power to stop the Confederacy from obtaining allies across the Atlantic Ocean. Times were turbulent during this period of world history. National governments were changing hands frequently. The fear that the Confederate States would be able to side with one of these factions was a reality. The image of the Confederacy needed to be corrected, from the one which Union diplomats and the liberal press in New York were slinging around, to a more civilized and well-mannered culture and persona. This was to be achieved by using the tactic *of **psychological warfare*** against the Union slanderers; *the planned use of propaganda and other psychological actions having the primary purpose of influencing the opinions, emotions, attitudes, and behavior of hostile nation groups in such a way as to support the achievement of national objectives.*[82] This warfare was conducted by the agents of the Secret Navy and those that were supporting her actions both directly

---

[82] Department of the Army, *FM 1-02 (FM 101-5-1) Operational Terms and Graphics*, 1-153.

and indirectly through other means than what their government was willing to do.

On 18 January 1863, Confederate President Jefferson Davis appointed James M. Mason as a commissioner "on call" to act on the Confederate government's behalf with other nations. This "other" nation would be the British Empire. [83] James M. Mason (*right*) was a former United States Senator from Virginia.

And once Virginia seceded, like many others, he left with her.[84] It was the hope of President Davis that embarking on a quayside embargo of cotton shipments to the European nations would motivate them to take action on officially recognizing the Confederate government, siding with her, and supporting her both militarily and financially if needed.[85] Things began to worsen in Europe, and

---

[83] Official Records of the Union and Confederate Navies in the War of the Rebellion by United States. Navy Dept, 31.

[84] "Intelligence in the Civil War."

[85] Frank L. Owsley Sr., *King Cotton Diplomacy: Foreign Relations of the Confederate States of America Paperback,* (Tuscaloosa, AL: University Alabama Press, 2008), 25-51.

there was hope that both Britain and France would rise up in anger and support the Confederate government soon; all because of cotton shortage. Especially since both countries were weary of the Union government and the illegal blockade, as perceived by most Europeans.[86]

Commissioner Mason was hoping and counting on the southern victories in early 1862 as their *"check"* in a possible *"check mate"* of a European alliance. With every attempt, Mason tried to get the British Parliament and Queen Victoria to "join forces" with the Confederate government and put an end to the blockade. This, he surmised, would open up trading with the Confederacy; and ease the cotton delinquency that was being felt by Her Majesty's subjects. The following dispatches from *The Public Life and Diplomatic Correspondence of James M. Mason*, demonstrate what Mason was up against:

---

[86] Lynn M. Case and Warren F. Spencer, *The United States and France Civil War Diplomacy,* (Philadelphia: University of Pennsylvania Press, 1970), 126-157.

Chapter 4 Secret Navy

" 24 Upper Seymour Street,
" Portman Square,
" February 16, 1863.

" *The Right Hon. Earl Russell,*
" *Her Majesty's Secretary of State*
" *For Foreign Affairs.*

" My Lord: I deem it incumbent upon me to ask the attention of Her Majesty's Government to recent intelligence received here in regard to the blockade in Galveston, in the State of Texas, and at Charleston, in the State of South Carolina.

* " First, as regards Galveston, it appears that the blockading squadron was driven from that port and harbor by a superior Confederate force, on the first day of January last; one ship of that squadron was captured, the flagship destroyed, and the rest escaped, making their way, it is said, to some point on the Southern coast occupied by the United States forces. Whatever blockade of the port of Galveston, therefore, may have previously existed, I submit was effectually raised and destroyed by the superior forces of the party blockaded.

" Again, as respects the port of Charleston—through the ordinary channels of intelligence we have information, uncontradicted, that the alleged blockade of that port was in like manner raised and destroyed by a superior Confederate force, at an early hour on the 31st of January ultimo, two ships of the blockading squadron having been sunk, a third escaped disabled, and what remained of the squadron afloat was entirely driven off the coast.

" I have the honour to submit, therefore, that any alleged pre-existing blockade of the ports aforesaid was terminated at Galveston on the 1st of January last, and at Charleston on the 31st of the same month—a principle clearly stated in a letter I have had the honor to receive from your Lordship, dated on the 10th instant.

" I am aware that official information of either of these events may not yet have reached the Government of Her Majesty; but the consequences attending the removal of the blockade (whether to be renewed or no) are so important to the commercial interests involved, that I could lose no time in asking that such measures may be taken by Her Majesty's Government in relation thereto as will best tend to the resumption of a commercial intercouse so long placed under restraint.

· " I avail myself of this occasion to acknowledge the receipt of your Lordship's letter of the 10th of February instant, to which I shall have the honor of sending a reply in the course of a day or two, and am

" With great respect, etc.,

" J. M. MASON,
" *Special Commissioner of the Confederate States of America.*"

"FOREIGN OFFICE, February 16th, 1863.

"SIR: I have the honor to acknowledge the receipt of your letter of this date, calling my attention to the occurrences, as reported in the public prints, at Galveston and Charleston on the 1st and 31st of January respectively, and I have the honor to inform you that your letter shall be considered by Her Majesty's Government.

"I have the honor to be, etc.,

"RUSSELL.

"*J. M. Mason, Esqr.*"

"DEPARTMENT OF STATE,   .

"RICHMOND, May 30th, 1863.

"*J. M. Mason, Esqr.*

"SIR: Since my No. 22, of 13th instant, I have received your No. 33, of 9th instant. Nos. 28, 30, 31, and 32 are still missing.

"I am happy to inform you of the full approbation accorded by the President to your action in the matter of the loan as explained in that dispatch.

"I have, through Mr. Hotze, received several copies of the '*Blue-Book*' containing your correspondence with Earl Russell on the subject of the blockade, and have some comments to make, and some further evidence to be placed before his Lordship, including extracts from his own correspondence, which fully corroborate our assertion that the blockade is ineffective and is respected by the British Government on grounds entirely independent of the intrinsic merits of the question. But I defer further remarks till I have received your dispatch covering the correspondence, as it may contain matter which would affect our action on the subject.

"I am very respectfully
"Your obedient servant,

"J. P. BENJAMIN."

Mason, receiving information collected within the States and transferred via the Richmond Line, sent correspondence in the same manner. One name mentioned in correspondence, deserving mention for his propaganda in support of the Southern effort in Europe, was Henry Hotze, *"The Mad Hatter"*.

The only reason he is referred to in this manner is because of his ideology and outlandish writings in an attempt to "motivate" the populace of Europe. As a former United States foreign service officer, he had considerable connections throughout Europe. His first trip to Europe was as a free-lance writer and propagandist for the Southern cause. This morphed into the Confederate government's attempt to gain popularity with the European populace.

Though an eloquent writer and speaker, Hotze was quite the racist. And as such, he attempted to legitimize the Southern cause by defending the institution of slavery. The underlying problem with his propaganda was that it was decidedly wrong. Hotze had made the Southern cause a defense of slavery, which is immoral, rather than a defense of States' rights, which is just and constitutional. Besides, European nations had already pronounced slavery illegal. Hotze's attempts at justifying slavery was, simply a red herring. Further, it was a total loss of time, money, and resources. A far better approach, one which Hotze was completely unsuited, would have concentrated on the illegal actions of President Lincoln against the Confederacy, going beyond the legal limits of the executive branch of the United States Constitution, striking portions of it outright to serve his own personal agenda.

Making overtures to the French was John Slidell. Being a former US Senator from Louisiana, as well as General P.T. Beauregard's brother-in-law, he was an obvious choice for Commissioner to his Majesty Napoleon III.[87] This meant that he, like Mason, was skilled in his ability to speak and play within the political battlefield. Due to the illicit arms dealing he was involved with, Slidell was the veritable *Han Solo* of the Confederacy. Sauvé and sly, Slidell proved perfect for arms dealings with France. Slidell gave a French agent $25,000 worth of "Secret Funds" to persuade newspaper and journal writers to defend the Southern response to the War of Northern Aggression. He was also able to hire a number of writers in London to write and publish on the South's behalf; because Mason refused to partake in illegal actions, only by diplomatic means, was his choice.[88] If a princess were to tell him, "I love you", there is no doubt he would answer with, "I know".

"Showing them compassion may be the only way to earn peace..."
– Captain James T. Kirk

The glory of the high seas, it will call many men in their youth to the navy, so that the "sea water may fill their veins".

What do commerce raiders have to do with the Confederate Secret Service? It was a clandestine enriched organization that created the commerce raiders and the blockade runners. These ships did not merely appear out of thin air, they had to be

---

[87] "Intelligence in the Civil War", 37.

[88] Ibid, 37-38.

produced. The process involved has been described with much detail. However, without the commerce raiders and blockade runners, the Richmond Line would have ceased to exist, because there would have been no raiders to support it.

Some men and their feats are rarely mentioned, and if any are, it is because of the foe's victory. Is it not easy to forget? Just as *it is easier to destroy than to create*, as Commander Spock once said? One such individual whose exploits preach such inaccuracies, never given great credit in any manner, is Raphael Semmes, aka *"Old Beeswax"*[89]. He was a Confederate Naval officer, and inarguably the most famous. He was a Marylander that was once an officer in the United States Navy. [90] Once the Southern states broke away from the Union one-by-one, so did Semmes. He resigned his commission in the United States Navy and headed by train to Montgomery, AL, where he sought out and was granted a commission in the Confederate Navy, which did not yet exist.[91]

Semmes was an innovator like many others involved within the "spy" networks of the War Between the States. After he received his commission from the Confederacy, a motivated Semmes was ready to go defeat the Yankee invader's Navy, and rid the seas of their tyrannical dealings. However, as he looked out into the water of the Gulf of Mexico he saw no ship. That's because at the time the Confederacy did not yet have any.

His first task as a Confederate Naval Commander

---

[89] de Kay, 80.

[90] Thomas, 182.

[91] *Confederate Raider Raphael Semmes*, (April 22, 2014, C-Span 3).

was to take a train north and purchase arms and munitions to bring back to Montgomery. An odd request, but he took it and ran with it, returning to Montgomery with the requested supplies. This odd request came from the highest authority, President Jefferson Davis.[92]

Still, there was no Navy, or for that matter, a ship for this sea fearer. Undaunted, Commander Semmes  (left) took matters into his own hands. He purchased the Confederate Navy's first vessel with his own money. This ship, an old mailer, the *Habana*, was to be the first commerce raider, the *CSS Sumter*.[93] This ship was not the amazing vessel that his other ships in the future would come to be, but it was a quick solution to an agonizing problem. There were some great unknown aspects about Commander Semmes. First, he had practiced law, which effected how he fought on the high seas. Each time his ships captured another vessel, he would look over their books and charter. If the ship was charted under a foreign country, and not under the United States of America, he would

---

[92] *Confederate Raider Raphael Semmes.*

[93] Thomas, 183.

release all; the ship, crew and cargo to continue on their venture. Second, he would ensure that after the initial engagement, no one was harmed. However, if the ship was a Union ship, the cargo would be confiscated. The crew was allowed to either join his crew, or remain as a prisoner aboard his ship until a neutral port was reached, and the vessel was burned. [94] Under Semmes' command, his most famous ship was the *290* aka *Enrica,* aka *CSS Alabama. Old Beeswax* was the scourge of the Union Navy and Lincoln's cabinet, due to his commerce raiding. The Union labeled him and his men as *"pirates"* to make their actions illegal; a recurring theme.

Other than officers, the crew of the CSS Alabama were comprised mainly of Europeans. This was due primarily to the fact she was built in England and never anchored in a Southern port. Foreign ports were always full of men looking for adventure and work as sailors. In 1864, upon leaving the port of Cherbourg, France, the Alabama sailed out to meet the Union cruiser, *USS Kearsarge.*[95] This battle was the talk of the continent. People from England boarded yachts, while those in France boarded trains from Paris to watch from the shore, or chartered boats to get even closer. Commander Semmes eventually lost his great ship in a little over an hour of fierce battle, and would go on to command the

---

[94] *Confederate Raider Raphael Semmes.*

[95] Stephen Fox, *Wolf of the Deep: Raphael Semmes and the Notorious Confederate Raider CSS Alabama,* (New York: Knopf Doubleday Publishing Group, 2009), 258-259.

James River squadron till the end of the war.[96]

After the war, Semmes was elected to be a judge in Mobile, AL, but the United States, still bitter about what he did during the war, thwarted his installation. Later, when Semmes attempted to practice law again, that too was impeded. Finally, Semmes was able to find a professorship at Louisiana State University in Baton Rouge, LA.

The *pirate* title stuck to Semmes and his men until the CSS Alabama Association provided evidence to the United States State Department that the *Alabama* was commissioned as a warship, therefore its crew and the ship should be treated as such. The State Department agreed, and now the *CSS Alabama* is protected.[97] Semmes and his daring exploits are now becoming famous in history, but only by those that agree it happened; because there are still those in the modern world that believe that Semmes' exploits are only propaganda, and his accomplishments never actually took place. Under his command, the *CSS Alabama* was able to travel over 75,000 miles in just under two years and capture sixty-four prizes under sail and steam.[98] Quite the achievement for a man that helped start a regular Navy that would become a secret one.

---

[96] John Bowman, *Chronicles of the Civil War: An Illustrated and Encyclopedia of America's Bloodiest War,* (North Dighton, MA: World Publications, 2005), 354.

[97] *Confederate Raider Raphael Semmes.*

[98] Allan R. Millett and Peter Maslowski, *For the Common Defense: A Military History of the United States of America,* (New York: Macmillian Press, 1984), 213.

Chapter 4 Secret Navy

"Wind to a sailor is what money is to life on shore."
– Sterling Hayden

Another covert agency taking part in Secret Navy Operations was the *Richmond Line*. Falling under the Department of the CS Navy, this courier system was used by the Secret Navy and agencies within the Secret Service Bureau, the Special and Detached Service, and Signal Corps. George N. Sanders perfected and maintained the line that was, early in 1860 known as the *Doctor Line*, then it merged with the *Maryland Line*, and finally becoming the *Richmond Line* or "*Secret Line*" as some prefer to call it. This line consisted of the various couriers within the States, territories, provinces, and countries already described. What is normally not thought of is that the actual post was moved via the *Richmond Line* through the normal postal system from Richmond to Washington or Baltimore. Confederate agents used this system in each respective location throughout the duration of the war because their lives depended on it. Therefore what must be remembered is that it is true that messages were moved via the *Richmond Line,* but common sense, would tell us that personnel working in a *permissive* environment would also elect to use the regular postal system. Not to mention, there were agents working in each post system respectively that could ensure the post moved effectively.

John H. Reagan, of Texas, was commissioned as the Confederate Post Master General. Reagan had served as a congressman for the State of Texas and his appointment was viewed by some as a "polite" gesture to appease the other States.

In reality, President Jefferson Davis appointed Reagan because he liked him and Texans liked him. He was the only member of Jefferson's cabinet that actually ran his office efficiently. He gave notice to the Confederate States when post service was going to be assumed by the Confederate mail system. He recruited postmasters in northern States with Southern heritage to join the South, which he did successfully, and he had his agents obtain all the paperwork they could from their Union post offices before they left so he had a blueprint to follow for 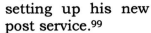 setting up his new post service.[99]

Under the guise of Postmaster General, Reagan (left) conducted himself as a true government official, all the while assisting the Confederate Secret Service Bureau and Signal Corps. This was done because the mail that was sent, sometimes with "secret" underlying messages, could be accomplished efficiently through the regular mail system. This would ensure that the information would travel fast and reach its actual destination. Confederate citizens were probably enthused that the mail system was not being run by another person, say like Braxton

---

[99] Thomas, 77-78.

Bragg. Another interesting bit of information about Reagan is that with the fall of the Confederate government in 1865, he and Governor Francis Lubbock of Texas were with President Jefferson Davis when he was arrested by Union soldiers in Georgia. It can be surmised that John Reagan was working with the Secret Service Bureau, possibly, because he was still traveling with Jefferson via the Richmond Line. Also, this brings up the question of why was Governor Lubbock there; and were these two men also members of the Canadian Bureau? It just doesn't make sense, and there is no such thing as a coincidence, especially during times of war. The speculation and links will be surmised in a later chapter. Let's look at a simple example of how it would have worked for the Richmond Line, the Secret Navy, and the Confederate Post System to work together to get a message out, and the reply back tying this all together. *Remember this is just a hypothetical example, but the names, locations, and jobs are factual.*

Secretary of War Judah P. Benjamin needs to get vital intelligence to James Bulloch in London on Union agents making their way to Europe. Benjamin's letter leaves Richmond bound in an envelope through the Confederate mail system to Alexandria, VA. There it is delivered to Edward Delcher aka Benjamin Franklin Stringfellow. Once in his hands, he would transfer the letter to Union post and have it mailed to an agent in Washington City to add to its validity. In Washington City, the next Confederate agent would receive the message, James H. Surratt. Now, being a Canadian Bureau Agent, Surratt delivers the letter himself to Reverend Stuart Robinson in Toronto. The Reverend then passes it off to the next Canadian Agent in line, Ms. Beverly Tucker who took a Canadian passenger ship, under the British flag, to Liverpool. There she would be met by J.R. Thompson who would pass the letter to James Bulloch.

Once Mr. Bulloch read the information he would have the intelligence sent to Confederate Commissioner James M. Mason, who at once would inform Lord Russell of the outrageous Union attempt that is going to take place and seeks assistance from Her Majesty's Government. To send back across the ocean exactly what had transpired since receiving the letter, Bulloch would have Thompson hand the letter off to Captain John Newland Maffitt aboard the *Owl*. Captain Maffitt would carry the letter in hand, during which time, he would run the Union blockade and arrive safely in port in Wilmington, NC. From there, he would pass the answer from Bulloch off to a Signal Corpsman, who would transmit the information to Mr. Myers in New Bern, NC. Mr. Myers would then give the letter to the 8th North Carolina Partisan Rangers to have it personally delivered to the Secretary of War Judah P. Benjamin in Richmond VA.

That was a hypothetical, but realistic way the Secret Navy operated using the other various organizations; and perfected the use of the Richmond Line. This same line of communication was also used to smuggle people and equipment across enemy lines. The Richmond Line would end up causing a great deal of controversy and was the subject of ridicule. The members of this line were involved in more operations then most people even care to speak of, or have just chosen to forget. Some of the members of the Richmond Line were innovative individuals that were looking at ways to change the face of warfare by seeking out new ways to conduct it. There is also speculation that the men within the Line were members of various organizations. What also has to be remembered is not all of the Richmond Line agents were born and reared Southerners. Northern individuals with Southern sympathies also manned the Line and assisted as agents in the operations.

Was there speculation that the Richmond Line was just a cover for the escape route of the famous assassin John Wilkes Booth? Yes, because within the Richmond Line there is historically nested evidence, that most, if not all of those involved in the plot were agents of the Confederate Secret Service Bureau and Signal Corps (diagram page 96). Can one start assuming that this is true and that the Confederate government was behind the assassination because they saw a documentary on television or YouTube? Sure, why not, but let's look at the facts before the finger pointing starts. It is easier to accuse later, rather than acquit, after facts have been presented.

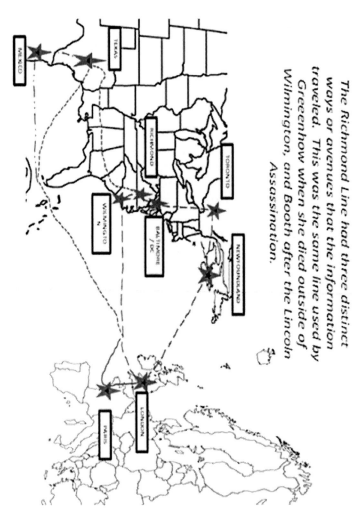

Note:

The Richmond Line had three distinct ways or avenues that the information traveled. This was the same line used by Greenhow when she died outside of Wilmington, and Booth after the Lincoln Assassination.

Figure 4-3. The Richmond Line.

Chapter 5
Oh, Canada

"I'm a Canadian ... It's all about maple syrup, not war."
– Leslie Feist

The War of Northern Aggression was taking a turn for the worse for the Confederacy late in 1863. President Davis was wondering how much longer his fellow countrymen were going to be able to repel the Yankee invader. There were, however, some operations being planned beyond the Union's northern border that Davis was counting on; and these were handled by the Secret Service Fund and Canadian Bureau. What has to be remembered is Canada was a territory of Great Britain, recognized simply as British North America, until she became an independent nation on 1 July, 1867. Therefore, it can be surmised that the reason Canada was so willing to assist the Confederacy was because she was simply an offshoot of her British parents on the North American continent.

On 6 February, 1863, the Confederate States of America Congress passed a resolution that stated, *"A secret agent should be sent to Canada to promote the above policy (which was formal recognition of the Confederacy by the United States government and an end to the war). That a sum of ___ dollars be placed at the disposal of the President to be used as a secret service fund for the purpose contemplated in these resolutions.*"[100] This bureau will become the most controversial of all of the detachments and organizations that dealt with clandestine, overt, or covert operations for and under the direct supervision of the Confederate government; and are still debated today by historians.

The man chosen to head up operations in Canada was Captain Thomas Henry Hines. He was personally selected by President Jefferson Davis, more than likely, because of his recent fame and abilities to evade if necessary; a beneficial quality for future operatives. Born and raised in Kentucky, Thomas Henry Hines was a member of John H. Morgan's Cavalry detachment. Riding with Morgan, Hines learned the art of scouting and intelligence gathering. He became famous when he and General Morgan escaped from a penitentiary in Ohio where they were being held captive by Union soldiers. Although a man of small stature, Hines was aptly described as having, *"blue eyes, black hair, athletic, and capable of endurance"*, [101] which meant that he was a short skinny energetic guy. What Hines had to do was organize each of the different organizations that fell under his direct command and simultaneously work with other entities outside of his jurisdiction.

One such organization, *that Hines is said to have been a member of,* was the Knights of The Golden

---

[100] "Journal of the Congress of the Confederate States of America, 1861 to 1865 Volume 6," Confederate States of America Congress, 81.

[101] John W. Headley, *Confederate Operations in Canada and New York,* (Honolulu: University Press of the Pacific, 2003), 217.

Circle. [102] As soon as anyone "hears" the word "Knights" mentioned within an organization, they begin to think about the Knights Templar, the movie *"National Treasure"*, the Masons, etc., when in reality there was more to them. Were they a group associated with the Masons? Some historians, writers, and investigators have said, "yes" due to the rituals they performed during the initiation process into the clique. However, as soon as they are labeled as such, then what they were really attempting to do is lost. Before this group is discussed, let's look into the Canadian Bureau.

As previously discussed, there were three distinct detachments in the Canadian Bureau: Canadian Operations Detachment, the Operation Stations, and the Northwest Confederacy (also called the Northwest Conspiracy). Each had their distinct area of operations, with left and right limits. The primary responsibilities of the Operation Stations were; to serve as base stations for meetings, handle the transfer of operational funds, provide and maintain residential structures to serve as safe houses for agents, disseminate plans if needed, and the storage of supplies and material. The purpose of the Canadian Operations Detachment was to conduct sabotage and subversion across the border into the United States. The Northwest Confederacy was funded and supported by the Canadian Bureau, but served more as the operational name for a plan devised by the Knights of the Golden Circle and the Sons of Liberty. The Sons wore on the lapels of their

---

[102] "Camp Douglas Conspiracy of 1864: The Northwestern Confederacy," accessed July 7, 2013, http://campdouglas.compuliance.com/camp-douglas-conspiracy-of-1864-the-northwestern-confederacy/.

jackets, the head of Liberty from a copper penny, and served as the action arm of the Copperheads. Copperheads were northern Democrats who sought out an end to the War of Northern Aggression by any means possible. To them, that meant the overthrow of the United States government and ending the conflict. This was a very radical group of individuals that were allied with the Confederacy.

> *"Canada is not the party. It's the apartment above the party."*
> *– Craig Ferguson*

Thomas H. Hines may have been the individual in charge of the Canadian Bureau, but there were three other men that were in command. For example, in the modern United States Army, a Commissioned Officer is in command of the unit, but generally, it is the Senior Non-Commissioned Officer who is in charge. In other words, Hines ran the day to day operations ensuring success, whereas the other three gentlemen handled the bureaucratic aspects and monies associated with the post. These other men that have been referred to were appointed by President Jefferson Davis as commissioners to Canada.

One was Jacob Thompson of Mississippi who was the former Secretary of the Interior under President Buchanan, and chief of all operations. The second commissioner was Clement Clay of Alabama, a former U.S. Senator, and lastly, James P. Holcomb of Virginia.[103] Clay, who had been waiting for a perfect post within the Confederate government, was a

---

[103] James D. Horan, *Confederate Agent: A Discovery in History*, (New York: Crown Publishers, Inc., 1954), 80-81.

reluctant covert agent, believing his posting well below his abilities. Clay confided in Texas Senator Louis Wingfall, *"It is a very difficult and delicate duty, for which I am not suited by my talents, tastes or habits. I cannot enjoy secret service. I have accepted it with extreme reluctance."[104]*

However, unlike Clay and the other commissioners, Hines was looking forward to getting at the Union and using the rebellious Copperheads to his advantage to wreak havoc across the Northwestern portion of the United States of America. Now, the next thing for these men to do was to organize as best they could and begin operations in an attempt to salvage a lost war against a northern aggressor.

The people that are often forgotten about are not the operatives themselves conducting clandestine, sabotage, or subversive operations, but the auxiliary that supported them through the process. Without an able auxillary, operations are rarely successful. Two such individuals had safe houses in Toronto. One was Mr. Withers (originally from Covington, Kentucky) who operated a boarding house in Toronto; [105] and the other was Reverend Stuart Robinson, who arrived in Toronto in 1863, and operated the Queens Hotel. Rev. Robinson was a dear friend of Doctor Blackburn,[106] who remained in

---

[104] "Clay to Texas Senator Louis Wingfall, April 29, 1864," The Clays of Alabama, (Lexington: University of Kentucky Press, 1958), 232.

[105] Headley, 215.

[106] Nancy Disher Baird, *Luke Pryor Blackburn: Physician, Governor, Reformer,* (Lexington, KY: The University of Kentucky Press, 1979), 26.

Toronto until 1866 when he returned to Louisville, KY. [107] Interesting enough, there is no other documentation noting that Rev. Robinson, who was a political refugee, was connected with Dr. Blackburn. One possibility for this lack of documentation may be that either Rev. Robinson, or his family deliberately sought to cover up the relationship. Men such as Rev. Robinson enabled Canadian operatives to have a place to hide out and seek refuge when needed.

While the Canadian Bureau was busy planning operations, the Union Secret Service began to infiltrate the Confederacy's Secret Service Bureau by conducting counter-espionage operations. When the war started, the Union was behind the power curve in regards to intelligence collection operations, but by 1863, had caught up quickly. The Canadian Bureau was behind numerous acts of sabotage and subversion; some successful, some not. Their targets included many cities to include: St. Albans, VT; New York City, NY; Boston, MA; Philadelphia, PA; Washington City; and Norfolk, VA. All of the targets, except two, were acts of *subversion*. In Washington City, for instance, Lincoln was the primary target.

The St. Albans Raid in Vermont was conducted on 19 October, 1864. It was a retaliatory attempt to answer the atrocities being conducted by General Sherman in the Southern States. Lieutenant Bennett H. Young was the man that led this operation. He was a recent escaped prisoner-of-war (POW) and

---

[107]"Kentucky: A History of the State, Perrin, Battle, Kniffin, 8th ed., 1888, Jefferson Co." accessed July 21, 2013, http://www.rootsweb.ancestry.com/~kygenweb/kybiog/jefferson/robinson.s.txt.

recruited several other escapees to take part in his plan that was sanctioned by Clay, via Canada.[108]

The plan was to loot the small, quaint, isolated town of St. Albans, VT, and burn it to the ground just as Sherman was doing in the South. Young had in his possession a concoction contained within bottles that was to assist their efforts to burn the town. It was known as *Greek Fire*, a petroleum-based incendiary concoction invented by the Byzantines.[109] He had his troopers arrive at different times by various means of transportation, so as not to draw suspicion. This raid was to serve as a test bed for future raids that were planned to be conducted throughout the northern part of the United States.

Having arrived early in Montreal, Lieutenant Young had a Confederate grey uniform, tailor made complete with a yellow stripe down the pant leg, signifying he was a cavalry officer.[110] The assailants made their way to the St. Albans bank, where one of the men, Tom Collins informed the bank teller, while pointing two Colt pistols, *"We are Confederate soldiers...We have come to give you a taste of Sherman's idea of war"*, and made everyone in the bank take an oath and swear allegiance to the Confederate States of America or be shot.[111] One has to imagine how upset the soldiers and people of the

---

[108] Adam Mayers, *Dixie & The Dominion: Canada, the Confederacy, and the War for the Union,* (Toronto: Dundurn Press, 2003), 115.

[109] "Greek Fire," accessed April 4, 2013, http://www.britannica.com/EBchecked/topic/244571/Greek-fire.

[110] Mayers, 105.

[111] Mayers, 10.

South were after reading, or hearing by word of mouth, how Sherman was conducting warfare sanctioned by Lincoln. It is only logical that they sought retaliation.

The men were able to rob three banks for a total of $200,000 and only burn a single shed, because their *Greek Fire* was not as potent as they had expected.[112] Once across the border, the men involved were either captured or elected to turn themselves in. The United States government immediately protested against the raid and demanded that the men be extradited at once for trial. Sitting in the Montreal jail, the men were treated like heroes by the city dwellers. They were given food, wine, tobacco, and local papers to keep up with world events. Eventually a trial was held in Canada, and the magistrate decided that because they were in military uniforms during the raid it was an act of war, not an act of terrorism conducted by civilians.[113]

> ***"I have generally given people the worth of their money twice told."***
> *– P. T. Barnum*

25 November, 1864, the day after Thanksgiving, aka **Black Friday**, there was another act of subversion. This act involved the use of Greek Fire within the city of New York, which was called by Northern newspapers, *"A Vast and Fiendish Plot"*. Jacob Thompson was the creator of this plan and called on Colonel Robert Martin to lead this operation. He was able to recruit seven other men for

---

[112] "Intelligence in the Civil War."

[113] Mayers, 244.

a total of eight Confederate Canadian Bureau Agents (John Yeats Beall, Lt. John Headley, Lt. Ashbrook, and Cpt. Robert Cobb Kennedy), which called themselves the *Confederate Army of Manhattan.*[114]

These men were also using the fabled *Greek Fire* in their scheme, however the difference was that their conglomeration was developed by a chemist in Cincinnati. The chemist mixed phosphorous and carbon bisulphide; when exposed to air, would burst into flames. [115] Martin held the final operational meeting in the Central Park cottage at six in the evening on 26 November to finalize the plan. They were to burn down 19 hotels *(all of which they had thoroughly cased)*, as well as Niblo's Garden Theater, and P.T. Barnum's American Museum. With the operational tone set, this *Confederate Army of Manhattan* set out to execute their orders.

One by one the men threw their glass bottles full of the flammable liquid into the buildings. Julius Caesar was saying his lines at the Winter Garden when the smoke from the LaFarge Hotel next door began to seep into the theatre. Someone yelled fire, and the Superintendent of firemen, yelled that it came from a drunk and to continue on with the play in order to avert a crisis in the theatre. He abruptly moved to the basement to assist the stage hands that had already begun fighting the blaze.[116] The actors

---

[114] "Notorious Terrorist Attacks in New York City," accessed September 18, 2013, http://www.newyorktalksandwalks.com/nm/publish/news_42.html.

[115] "Intelligence in the Civil War", 45.

[116] Horan, 213-219.

performing the play were from a famous family, and one of their names would go down in history as a fiend. John Wilkes Booth, and his two brothers were in the Winter Garden performing the play *Julius Caesar* by William Shakespeare when the fire occurred.[117]

All of the Greek fires were set off as planned; however, little damage was inflicted and therefore, did not achieve the overall intent of massive panic. When the men met back up, they were curious to know how the newspapers had already printed out *"Extras"* of their plot with very detailed descriptions, to include mentioning the names of those involved. When Headley read in one paper, that one of their fellow agents, Godfrey Hyams, was really a Union informant, they knew they must leave at once and make their way back to Canada. Headley had provided Hyams with the details of their plans when they met in Canada, not knowing that their Greek Fires would have worked had the chemist not been "persuaded" by Hyams to "water down the solution" to limit its ability on the buildings.[118]

"But tonight, we will hurl the gauntlet of science into the frightful face of death itself. Tonight, we shall ascend into the heavens!"
– Dr. Frederick Frankenstein

---

[117] Sam Roberts, "As Booth Brothers Held Forth, 1864 Confederate Plot Against New York Fizzled," last modified November 24, 2014, http://www.nytimes.com/2014/11/25/nyregion/as-booth-brothers-held-forth-1864-confederate-plot-against-new-york-fizzled.html?_r=1.

[118] Horan, 220-221.

Chapter 5 Oh, Canada

An individual, rarely, if ever mentioned in history text concerning the Civil War, or any of the various secret societies, is Doctor Luke Pryor Blackburn. Some consider him to be more "evil genius" than a practitioner of medicine. Now, why such a harsh and rash title for a man considered to be a medical expert in his field of study? The answer lies in the way this Kentucky doctor used his knowledge of medicine to wage war on the United States of America. Dr. Blackburn is credited by some for being the first in recorded history to introduce a new type of warfare; biological warfare, also known as bioterrorism (in modern language). Was he really "evil", or was it the innovation itself that scared people. Were these alleged actions merely the defense of a nation at all costs?

Luke Pryor Blackburn was born on 16 June, 1816, in Woodford County, Kentucky, and was one amongst a family consisting of thirteen brothers and sisters. His family was a large, Southern, gentile family, and Blackburn was brought up with the luxuries of upper-class citizenship. Blackburn opened his own medical practice in Lexington, KY after graduating from Transylvania University Medical School in 1835 at the age of 18. Outbreaks of cholera were common during this time and Blackburn witnessed, first hand, the horrific aftermath of an epidemic. He also learned how to properly diagnose and treat various other communicable diseases that frequently ravaged the South.

His medical practice was well regarded, but like most country doctors with few patients, was not lucrative. He eventually moved his family to the sprawling river city, Natchez, Mississippi, for more opportunity and a better life. Blackburn managed the local hospital, became Natchez's elected health officer, and developed a friendship with his neighbor, the future President of the Confederacy, Jefferson Davis. Because of the boggy lowlands teeming with mosquitos, Natchez was susceptible to yellow fever, and it didn't take long for an epidemic to break out.[119]

Yellow fever, also known as "black vomit" due to its presentation of jaundice (yellow skin) and internal hemorrhaging, which accounts for the sufferers' characteristic dark vomit and stool, was a wasting and deadly virus that affected all ages, both rich and poor, and frequently resulted in death roughly ten days after initial infection. Despite fear of contagion, Blackburn treated the sick and dying with little regard for himself, treating patients for free despite the fact he had a wife and son to support.[120] He continued to practice medicine until the beginning of the War of Northern Aggression, or as British North Americans called it, *The Second American Revolution.*

Once war began, Blackburn did not join the military, most likely because he felt he was too old at age forty-five. He was not content to serve the South merely as a field surgeon, and was frustrated when his suggestion to serve as the General Inspector of Hospitals and camps, without pay, to the newly

---

[119] Jane Singer, *The Confederate Dirty War*, (Jefferson, NC: McFarland & Company, Inc., 2005), 82-83.

[120] Jackie Rosenhek, "The beginnings of bioterrorism, During the Civil War, Dr. Blackburn hatched a plan to use sickness as a weapon," last modified August 2008, http://www.doctorsreview.com/history/the-beginnings-of-bioterrorism/.

organized Confederate government was ignored. Doctor Blackburn finally received the type of wartime adventure he was interested in. He made a proposal to the Commander of Mobile that he desired to assist the blockade runners with needed supplies for the South, in exchange for protection at the gulf port when reached. There was to be no pay or monies exchanged, his only wish was to be allowed to sell ice he brought from Canada to cover his expenses. Governor Pettus of Mississippi approved the plan and appointed Blackburn as his agent in the Canadian Bureau. In August of 1863, Doctor Blackburn set off on a trip to Toronto that would change history, and later question who he had dealings with during his stay there.[121]

The "evil" or "notorious" Doctor Blackburn, as some historians have referred to him, devised a plan to use yellow fever to the South's advantage. Being the world's subject matter expert on the disease, he surmised that he would be able to take infected clothing from those with the disease and then transfer its lethal ability. It was believed, then, that the disease was transferred by bodily fluids such as sweat, and therefore contaminated clothing could be effective. What Blackburn and others didn't know then, was that yellow fever is a viral infection spread by a particular type of mosquito."[122] However, based on his assumptions of how the disease was

---

[121] Baird, 21.

[122] "Yellow Fever," accessed October 12, 2013, http://www.mayoclinic.org/diseases-conditions/yellow-fever/basics/definition/con-20032263.

transferred, he was willing to act to bring the Union to its knees, even if it meant bioterrorism.

In 1864, a horrible epidemic of yellow fever on the Island of Bermuda erupted. This was Doctor Blackburn's chance to make his move. He arranged to meet J.W. Harris in Halifax with eight trunks, five of which had clothing that were worn by patients inflicted with yellow fever. The plan was to have the clothing shipped to second hand stores in the United States where they would be purchased; and thus the disease would spread causing an epidemic in the North. [123] The trunks were transported aboard the *Alpha* by its captain W.J. Hall to Halifax where Harris was waiting. The *Alpha* was the same boat that transported Jacob Thompson, Clement Clay, and William W. Clearly to Canada. Harris received the trunks and took them to his hotel room where he repacked them; following Doctor Blackburn's strict rules to keep him from contracting the deadly disease by "chewing camphor and smoking strong cigars".[124] Hall and Harris were able to bribe a ship bound for the United Sates named the *Halifax* to transport the goods in the smugglers hold. Once in Boston with the trunks, Harris had them sent to Philadelphia, New York, Washington City (specifically trunk No. 2 which contained a package of a nice dress shirt inflicted with the disease bound for President Lincoln), and Norfolk.

The only problem that J.W. ran into was he couldn't get through the Union blockade to deliver the clothing to enemy occupied New Bern. Therefore,

---

[123] Baird, 24-25.

[124] Baird, 29.

he hired the services of a sutler by the name of Mr. Myers, to transport the clothing down there for him. Weeks later there was news of a massive outbreak of yellow fever in New Bern; so Harris figured that Myers had carried out his end of the bargain and the plan worked.[125] Also it is key to mention that J.W. Harris is the cover name for *Godfrey J. Hyams,* a Union agent that had shown his true colors in New York.

Hyams wasn't paid by Blackburn for services rendered when he reached Halifax. Enraged, he went to Blackburn's boss, Jacob Thompson where he gave a sob story of not being paid. He was finally paid, but there were other outlandish offerings he swore he was indebted to by promises made from Blackburn. When these were brushed aside, he went to the Union authorities about the plot. The United States, hearing of the plot and having a sworn affidavit from Hyams, wanted Blackburn extradited to the U.S. to stand trial, and moved the Canadian government to take action. On 19 May, 1865, Blackburn was arrested in Toronto. There were multiple speculations being made, and the biggest was an attempt to connect Blackburn with Booth and Davis.

The Union was calling for blood and they wanted to "see" the connection between the men. It was decided by the Canadian government that there was no proof that the trunks were ever on Canadian soil and therefore Doctor Blackburn was not in any violation of any neutrality act. The Union officials also threw out the claims against Blackburn because there was not enough evidence to convict him of any wrong doing. If they would have waited longer, there were still Confederate government papers being

---

[125] Baird, 29-30.

compiled in Richmond. One such letter was from
Rev. Stuart to President Davis. Stuart had been hired
by President Davis to conduct clandestine missions
at his disposal. The letter referred to Blackburn, but
not by name, and the act he was attempting with the
infected yellow fever clothing. It was a plea to stop
the trunks from being delivered as an act of
humanity.[126]

This letter was not found in time, but certainly
could have been used as evidence against Blackburn.
If this letter by Stuart to Davis had been found,
perhaps other testimony that Blackburn had met
with Booth in Montreal, both confirmed Canadian
Bureau Agents, would have stood up in court.[127] It
could be considered speculation, but Blackburn was
a Canadian Agent working with other Canadian
Agents, which has been proven. There is no logical
explanation on why he *wouldn't* have met with
Booth. Not to mention, if Blackburn was willing to
pass off a dress shirt, soiled with yellow fever, in
hopes of killing the President of the United States,
Abraham Lincoln, why not go all out when your first
plan didn't work? Stuart had the money. Blackburn
had the brains. How could it not be surmised, that
not only Blackburn, but Stuart also, played a pivotal
role in the assassination of Abraham Lincoln? Others
simply view Doctor Blackburn as generally a good
guy with a bad idea, and in 1867, Blackburn would

---

[126] Edward Steers, *Blood on the Moon: The Assassination of Abraham Lincoln,* (Lexington, KY: The University Press of Kentucky, 2005), 49-53.

[127] Baird, 32.

again set foot in his country, as a citizen of the United States of America.

However, because the conspirators had been hung and Davis had been acquitted, as was Blackburn, his actions were brushed under the rug. A man that attempted to use yellow fever to cause pandemonium throughout the North would never have to worry about people hearing about this in the future. Why would they? It was, as Doctor Blackburn himself put it, *"too preposterous for intelligent men to believe"*.[128] However, in all reality, Doctor Blackburn never took a life because the yellow fever virus is spread by a mosquito. Even though there were some, after the war, that attempted in vain to tarnish the good name of the future Governor of Kentucky, Luke Pryor Blackburn, he was loved in Kentucky just as Jefferson Davis was loved throughout the South after his release from prison. It is easy to point fingers, and why not?

Doctor Blackburn had an ingenious way to engage in warfare; and it would be used effectively during the Great War (World War One). It isn't until then, that historians and scholars first talk about bioterrorism or biological warfare. He was a man that

---

[128] Baird, 34.

-Dr. Blackburn is viewed by many to be an evil man because they are ill informed of what he did after the war. It is easier to keep or attempt to label him as an evil man than to accept what he did before and after the war. Take Wernher von Braun for instance, a man that created the dreadful V-2 rocket that killed many innocent civilians in England, however because of his contributions to the space race he is hailed as a hero and not a murderer. This is where the delineation of good versus evil has to be made and what happened in the past can be learned from but not dwelled upon. This is only done by those that wish to keep truth at bay and let fiction take hold as fact.

changed the world for the better by his many contributions, and attempted on one occasion to end a war early. Think about Robert J. Oppenheimer and what he accomplished during World War Two. His creation is viewed by some as horrendous (the atomic bomb) or evil, notorious; though his invention most likely saved many lives and ended a bloody war early. This may be exactly what Doctor Luke P. Blackburn was attempting to accomplish. The term *bioterrorism* is a label from those that write history with no regard to truth or accuracy, not by those that attempt to recollect it. The invader will be able to tell the story, not those conquered; political correctness ruins their memories.

"Open your minds, my friends. We all fear what we do not understand."
– Professor Langdon

History has, in recent times, come to accept the fact that the Knights of the Golden Circle (KGC) had a role to play in the development of the war. There is speculation that it was a sect that was wishing to undermine the world and create a *"new world order"*. It was really a fraternal organization of men that had a plan to resurrect the Confederacy in the event that the war was lost. Of course, if you're on the other side, you will automatically begin to say that the KGC was an evil organization, aimed at the overthrow of the American government in order to rule the world. Why wouldn't a Northerner say that? People fear what they don't understand. It is easy to delegitimize a group, and that has been proven throughout history.

This group called themselves the Knights of the Golden Circle because they were attempting to initiate a *"Golden Circle"*. The *Golden Circle (below)* was the area around the Gulf of Mexico, and was called as such because of the rich soil that it possessed for producing cash crops, mainly cotton.

If the KGC were successful procuring additional land, then the Confederacy would be able to rebuild, and make a bid for another war when the time was right. What does this have to do with the Canadian Bureau? To be sure, many of the KGC members were also agents within the Canadian Bureau and were all working together to form the Northwest Confederacy, along with the Sons of Liberty. This plan could be related to *"Manifest Destiny Confederate Style"*.[129]

Some members of the KGC were; John Wilkes Booth, Thomas Hines, Jessie James, John H. Surratt, Nathan Bedford Forrest, John Calhoun, Edwin Stanton *(Lincoln's Secretary of War)*, Albert Pike, and J.O. Shelby to name a select few. The Canadian Bureau was given $1 million from the Confederate government to finance the Northwest Confederacy. In addition, Quantrill's Raiders were

---

[129] "America Unearthed Season 2 Episode 12," History Channel, released February 15, 2014.

robbing Union paymasters of the soldiers' pay, stashing it throughout the Southern part of the now United States; and one of his top raiders was Jessie James, a confirmed KGC member.[130] The KGC was even hard at work even before the war began to secure the secession of the Southern states; in a preparatory movement.

As States across the South were debating within their respective congressional chambers on whether or not they should secede from the Union, the key task of the KGC, apparently, was to ensure the vote passed. One such instance occurred in Texas as lawmakers presented the vote to the people of the State in February 1861. The vote was to decide whether to remain loyal to the Union or join the separatist movement that was sweeping across the cotton belt. The KGC had already envisioned an invasion of Mexico via Texas to annex the country as part of the planned withdrawal from the Union in the spring of 1860. So this plot has to come as no surprise. Loyalists plead they were kept from the polls by KGC members, and their votes were not counted, which gave the State the required majority to approve secession. [131] Texas appears to have played a large role in the KGC because there are tunnels beneath many cities throughout the State. One such city is Brownwood, TX, where it is still

---

[130] "America Unearthed Season 2 Episode 12," History Channel, released February 15, 2014.

[131] Randolph B. Campbell, "KNIGHTS OF THE GOLDEN CIRCLE," Handbook of Texas Online (http://www.tshaonline.org/handbook/online/articles/vbk01), accessed May 14, 2014. Uploaded on September 19, 2010. Published by the Texas State Historical Association.

believed to this day, Jessie James resided there under the alias of *Henry Ford,* living off the money stashed in the tunnels beneath the city, placed there by the KGC.[132]

As far as the development of the Northwest Confederacy, a man named Clement L. Vallandigham  (left) was a significant player in this plot. Vallandigham, a former US Congressman from Ohio, was the Copperhead leader. He claimed that he had 300,000 Sons of Liberty ready at his call to help overthrow the Union occupied military and government posts within the Northwestern part of the United States (which at that time was Indiana, Illinois, Ohio, and Iowa, what is known today as the Mid-West). [133] This man was not quiet about where his loyalties may have been because, "*in 1863, soldiers arrested, tried and found guilty...Clement L. Vallandigham of Ohio for violating Army orders against public expressions of Confederate sympathies...denounced the War and the Administration at home and in Congress. President*

---

[132] America Unearthed Season 2 Episode 12.

[133] "Intelligence in the Civil War", 43.

Abraham Lincoln banished..."[134] Not only was he sent away to the South, but he made his way back into Ohio and used his exile as a rally cry against an unconstitutional act infringed upon by Lincoln. Additionally, during his exile, Vallandigham made his way to Canada (no surprise there) and received approval from the delegates of the Democratic Party to run for Governor of Ohio in 1863. However, he was defeated by 100,000 votes to a pro-Union sympathizer.[135]

It is simply amazing that while in another country, still exiled from the one he was running for public office in, Vallandigham was given the approval of his party at the State convention to run for the governorship. As well as knowing that he was a Southern sympathizer, many people in Ohio still voted for the man. If he would have won the election, it would have been disastrous for Lincoln and his attempt to keep States in the Union. Vallandigham and the Sons of Liberty would have been able to act on the Northwest Confederacy without having to fire a single shot, simply taking it from within by securing the powerful State seats of a democratic government.

Ohio was a hotbed for the Northwest Confederacy. Thomas Hines had already been making preparations for a raid of the entire State by General Morgan's Raiders in June of 1863. He did this by stealing Union uniforms and payroll trains, as well

---

[134] "EX PARTE VALLANDIGHAM," accessed 25 November 2014, http://www.oyez.org/cases/1851-1900/1863/1863_2.

[135] "Clement Vallandigham," accessed 25 November 2014, http://www.ohiohistorycentral.org/w/Clement_Vallandigham.

as supplies from sutlers, and emplacing caches throughout Indiana in preparation for the Ohio raid. While there, Hines met with Copperheads who were reluctant at the time to give approval of any military action to be taken in their State in support of the Confederate cause. He and his men were almost caught there by Union home guardsmen, but made it back to Kentucky meeting up with Morgan for the Ohio raid.[136]

The actions of the Canadian Bureau were numerous and had lasting effects on the outcome of the war. These men and women involved were conducting espionage at its finest; at the same time devising unthinkable new ways of conducting warfare, some of which was retaliatory in nature.

There is a line that connects all of the players of the Lincoln Conspirators to the members of the Confederate's Secret Service Bureau and Secret Service Fund Detachment. This could be a coincidence, but that is unlikely.

---

[136] Spencer C. Tucker, *American Civil War: The Definitive Encyclopedia and Document Collection,* (Santa Barbara, CA: ABC-CLIO, 2013), 913-914.

Chapter 6
Doctor Who

"Never ignore coincidence. Unless, of course,
you're busy. In which case, always ignore
coincidence."
– Doctor Who

There were numerous "doctors" that contributed to the Confederate war effort; some known for their abilities in the field hospitals, saving the lives of brave Confederate soldiers. These same doctors fill the pages of history books and placards at museums across the United States of America for all to see and read about. However, there are some "doctors", some real, others merely an alias, that few people know about because they aren't mentioned in the texts of modern history. Their many contributions apparently considered insignificant by "modern scholars". These "unknown" doctors, and sometimes their wives as well, contributed talents, other than medicine to the Confederate espionage web. Some of the actions of these doctors are considered notorious for what they either attempted or achieved, but nonetheless, deserve mention of their service during the War of Northern Aggression.

For instance, there was Doctor B__, the cover for Major Cornelius Boyle, Doctor Luke Pryor Blackburn, Doctor Richard M. Sykes, and Doctor Samuel Mudd, which have already been mentioned, therefore do not require an introduction. Not all of these men were actual "doctors"; some chose to use the professional title as their false persona, because it allowed them to move freely at night when questioned why they were out so late.

"I am and always will be the optimist. The hoper of far-flung hopes and the dreamer of improbable dreams."
– Doctor Who

There were many foreigners on both sides of the conflict. Some were *"Shanghaied"* by the Union government to fight Lincoln's war, but most foreigners came by choice, either before the war started, or during it.

One of these foreign born volunteers was Doctor William T. Passmore. He was born in England and came to Baltimore, MD as a child. It was there, in Baltimore, where he would earn his medical degree and begin to practice medicine.[137] Along with most Marylanders, Passmore felt loyalties to the South, and would aid her as he could in defense of the Confederate States of America. To him, that meant joining the military to fight. He first attempted to join Confederate General Loring in the mountainous regions of Virginia. But being a medical practitioner, his services were needed at the field hospital. While there, his unique talents were enlisted by General Robert E. Lee, who sent him to conduct an espionage mission directed against General Burnside's forces.

While conducting this mission, Passmore was recognized by a Union soldier as soon as he entered their lines, but continued without missing a beat, narrowly avoiding the close encounter. He figured he had to work on his disguise, and did with great

---

[137] Ella Lonn, *Foreigners in the Confederacy,* (Chapel Hill: UNC Press Books, 2002), 266.

craftiness. Passmore grabbed some old soiled rags and other bits of clothing he found on the ground, and wore them. He also procured a cart and loaded it with produce. The cover he was using was that of a derelict, mentally unstable old man selling items from his cart to make ends meet. [138] This disguise was so effective that General Burnside spoke openly, within earshot of Passmore, about his plans for an upcoming battle, and even provided Passmore with a daily pass allowing Passmore to come and go as he pleased through his lines. Within days, Passmore was able to not only collect, but also provide significant amounts of information to General Lee. With this vital intelligence, Lee was able to win the battle of Fredericksburg, which has been credited to the intelligence collected by Doctor William T. Passmore. [139]

General Braxton Bragg was not well-respected by many within the Confederacy. There is even talk that he may have suffered from a multiple personality disorder, which may explain his poor performance on the battlefield. Bragg was provided information from his lead intelligence collector, a scout by the name of Captain H.B. Shaw, aka "Doctor C.E. Coleman", of the Coleman Scouts. Captain Shaw provided Bragg vital intelligence on numerous accounts, up until the time he was captured and eventually sent to Johnson's Island. Fortunately, he was not hung

---

[138] Lonn, 266.

[139] Mike Henry, *What They Didn't Teach You in American History Class,* (Boulder, CO: R&L Education, 2014), 62.

because he wore the uniform of a confederate officer and therefore wasn't considered a "spy".[140]

His courier, Sam Davis, did not fare so well. He was apprehended by Union soldiers, and under his saddle were papers containing the composition and disposition of the Union army in middle-Tennessee, along with maps depicting fortifications, detailed reinforcement plans of the army in Chattanooga, and gifts from one "C.E. Coleman" to General Bragg. The Union commander believed that one of his men had given up the information, and they were trying to figure out who the "C.E. Coleman" was that signed the papers, even though Captain Shaw was already in Union custody. Davis was later hung because he was unwilling to divulge information concerning Doctor "C.E. Coleman's" true identity.[141]

Doctor Aaron Van Camp was a well-known dentist in the Washington City area, which made him an ideal person to collect intelligence on the Union. As an on-the-job-trained spy, what Van Camp lacked in street-craft, he made up for in zeal, albeit perhaps too zealous. Van Camp was the personal dentist of Rose O'Neal Greenhow.[142] One may conclude that Greenhow recruited him, since there is a reference that he was a member of the spy ring she was associated with[143]. However, there also exists a

[140] Francis Trevelyan Miller and Robert Sampson Lanier, *Soldier life, Secret Service,* (New York: Review of Reviews Company, 1912), 292.

[141] Markle, 23.

[142] Larry G. Eggleston, *Women in the Civil War: Extraordinary Stories of Soldiers, Spies, Nurses, Doctors, Crusaders, and Others,* (Jefferson, NC: McFarland & Company Inc., 2009), 14.

[143] Markle, 160.

reference that he acted alone.[144] Doctor Van Camp was eventually captured in 1861, when he was suspected of being an agent of the Confederate government collecting intelligence in Washington City, and was held at the Old Capital Prison. It didn't help him much that he also assisted a Union soldier in defecting from the Union to the Confederacy. As one can assume, the Union authorities were not happy with him.[145] He was eventually paroled but continued to conduct espionage missions, along with his son, who was a Confederate soldier that had been wounded in battle.

"Don't blink. Don't even blink. Blink and you're dead. Don't turn your back. Don't look away. And don't blink."
– Doctor Who

During the 1850s, there were many fledgling secret societies dedicated to State's rights and westward expansion located throughout the country. A man by the name of Doctor George W.L. Bickley (page 125) believed these societies needed to be revamped and better organized into a single organization. He founded and organized the Knights of the Golden Circle in 1854, establishing the first chapters (called castles) and headquarters in Scioto

---

[144] Wilson, 42.

[145] The War of the Rebellion: v. 1-8 [serial no. 114-121]
Correspondence, Orders By United States War Department, 572-574.

County and Cincinnati. [146] This man was a well-known doctor, and he should be since he possessed nearly every advanced degree known to man-kind. How was this possible? Well it is easy when each one is forged. However, besides being a legitimate phrenologist (study of the skull), he was a prolific writer and a notable speaker. Under his leadership, the KGC spread throughout the South and into portions of the northern United States.[147]

He was providing information and working on

organizing resistance movements to help create the Northwest Confederacy; and he was well known to Thomas Hines. The Doctor contributed as best he could up until he was arrested by Union Special Detectives (USD) on 17 July, 1864, in Louisville, KY. He would have been able to make a successful escape with the cover story he had developed, but *"Murphy"* had another plan. As fate would have it, within the confines of his luggage contained a message that was discovered when his luggage was searched before he could leave town. It contained, "a

---

[146] David C. Keehn, *Knights of the Golden Circle: Secret Empire, Southern Secession, Civil War,* (Baton Rouge, Louisiana State University Press, 2013) 8-9.

[147] Horan, 16.

secret code and the original brass plate seal of the Knights of the Golden Circle...small package of red dust...number of incriminating papers, and two small stars from a general's uniform which were being used as Copperhead symbols". He attempted to talk his way out of being arrested to no avail. He was thrown in the Federal Penitentiary at Columbus, OH, until October 1865, dying in 1867 of natural causes.[148]

French Lick, IN was home to Doctor William A. Bowles, who just happened to be the Copperhead leader in Indiana. Doctor Bowles worked feverishly to assist Thomas Hines and General Morgan in any way that he could to help with their portion of the Northwest Confederacy plan. He was fifty-five years of age in 1863, and was a veteran of the Mexican War where he served as a Colonel in the Second Indiana Volunteers; involved in the retreat at Buena Vista. Bowles was known by the Union counter-espionage detachments to be a Confederate sympathizer and equipped the Copperheads under his command with the best of weaponry in the event they had to take to arms.[149]

There were times when he would dispatch his own agents to Indianapolis to serve as an early warning if any Union detectives were on their way. One instance, thankfully for Hines, the Doctor had sent his agents as he always did, because one rider returned to his house to inform him that a posse of Union agents were enroute. They had been given information that Hines and his men were at Doctor

---

[148] Horan, 33-63.

[149] Ibid, 25-26.

Bowles house. When the Union agents arrived they only found Bowles and his wife in bed. Mrs. Bowles gave the Union men a tongue lashing while Doctor Bowles screamed obscenities at them into the night; as Hines and his men watched from the bushes across the road hidden from Yankee view.[150]

Eventually Colonel Henry B. Carrington of the Union detectives had enough, and he organized a massive arrest of several suspected and confirmed Copperhead leaders in Indiana. Bowles was tried before a military tribunal, but not before his wife had attempted to sneak him in a Bowie knife and $1,250 while incarcerated. During her visit, she was able to pass Doctor Bowles a note written in ancient Egyptian hieroglyphics, which informed him that men were armed and waiting to fight.[151] Bowles was found guilty by the jury and sentenced to death by hanging. Carrington notified Washington of the impending rebellion because there were thousands of armed men calling for his release. Just in the nick of time, Washington intervened and the men were handed over to the State of Indiana to serve life sentences.[152]

> **"Achieve? We're not achieving anything. We're just hanging, it's nice in here."**
> – *Doctor Who*

---

[150] Horan, 122.

[151] Ibid, 150.

[152] Ibid, 153.

One of the secret lines of communication used by the Confederacy was named the *Doctor Line;* named for the profession of its members. Doctor Stoughton Dent was a paid agent of the Confederate Secret Services. He conducted espionage in Washington, Baltimore, and New York. This intelligence was collected and sent Monday, Thursday, and Saturday of each week. [153] Doctor Edward H. Wyvill was another member of the original *Doctor Line.* He resided in the southern portion of Prince George County, VA, which was directly across from Doctor Dent who lived in Charles County, MD.[154] It can be assumed that these two men were well acquainted with each other.

There is still little known about some doctors that may have served the Confederate Secret Services. Two doctors, in particular, are believed to have been involved based on speculation of certain facts and trends. Augusta Morris, a Confederate espionage agent in Washington, was arrested and sent to the Old Capital Prison (page 129) when she was found in bed with the Adjunct General of the Union Army. Augusta Morris was a married woman, and her husband was a doctor from Virginia. Therefore, it is surmised that her husband, Doctor Morris, as well, was involved in the espionage operations within Washington City.[155]

---

[153] William A. Tidwell, *Come Retribution: The Confederate Secret Service and the Assassination of Lincoln,* (Jackson, MS: The University Press of Mississippi, 1988), 98.

[154] Tidwell, April '65, 67.

[155] Markle, 169.

Doctor C__, as he has come to be known, was married to Mary Watson. Mary Watson was an agent of the Confederacy and her house was used as a signal station for agents waiting to know if there were Union soldiers in the area before traveling. It is said she married Doctor C__, which was Clement C. Watson; a Major and very famous blockade runner for the South. There is very little published about him, and no stories or tales of his exploits.[156]

The doctors that assisted the Confederate cause did so under the hope of defending a way of life that they believed in. Some were better than others at their job of espionage; while others were careless. There were *real* doctors, and doctors *in name only*, purely used as a false persona or cover. Each one of these men were supported by their loved ones, and if lucky, served right alongside them as they battled against the "evil" Union, as they viewed it.

The war was not fought on dry land only, and some men were busy designing and developing weapons of war for the high seas, ports, and rivers through innovative thinking and trial and error.

Old Capital Prison ca 1863.

---

[156] Charles Elisha Taylor, *The Signal and Secret Service of the Confederate States,* (Hamlet, NC: Capital Printing CO., 1903), 22.

Chapter 7
Polytechnic Corps

"I wish to have no connection with any ship that does not sail fast for I intend to go in harm's way."
– Captain John Paul Jones

Controlling waterways is nothing new in warfare, and Americans too, have our own history with regards to our attempts to do the same. Whether it was the American Revolutionaries placing a chain across the Hudson River to keep British ships from attacking West Point, or the Union sinking of older vessels in the port of Charleston, SC, all changed the course of history in some way, shape or form. The Confederacy was no different than her Union counterparts in wanting to limit the advancement of the enemy through vital waterways. The Secret Service Bureau needed a detachment to work on this issue, and the man selected to lead the effort would be Brigadier General Gabriel Rains of New Bern, North Carolina.

Rains, who had served in the Seminole and Mexican Wars, was commissioned a general by recommendation from President Jefferson Davis once he enlisted. He was a well-respected man and soldier, and a West Point graduate. He was assigned to serve as the garrison commander in Yorktown, VA. Each and every day he drilled his men for battle. One fateful day, there was a chance of being overrun and the city taken by General McClellan's army. In order to bolster his defenses, he planted what was to be the grizzly future of warfare, land mines. The reason he decided to use his invention was to slow down the Union advance, allowing his men time to seek refuge outside of the city. His new weapon worked and took several Union lives in the process. Generals Longstreet and Johnston were appalled by the use of this "un-Christian" weapon. However, when approval for its use in waterways was given by the

Confederate War Department, General Lee called on General Rains *(left)* to mine the James River. [157] After being severely wounded at the Battle of Seven Pines, Rains was transferred to the Cape Fear District to continue his work.[158]

On 31 October 1862, the Polytechnic Corps was created.[159]

---

[157] "Brigadier General Gabriel J. Rains: Father of Modern Mine Warfare," accessed 2 August 2014, http://gabrielrains.com/confederate-service/.

[158] Craig Pippen, "Gabriel James Rains Bio-Sketch," Camp 2205, Stem, NC, last modified January 2014, http://www.ncscv.org/gabriel-james-rains.

[159] David Winfred Gaddy.

In December of 1862, Rains was given the command of the Volunteer and Conscript Bureau, which was renamed the Torpedo Bureau. [160] Brigadier General Rains was to command the Polytechnic Corps, which under his watch was the newest detachment of the Secret Service Bureau. At first it was only concerned with torpedo manufacturing, but soon it was to include the Submarine Battery Service.[161]

"I need something stronger than tea."
– Sherlock Holmes

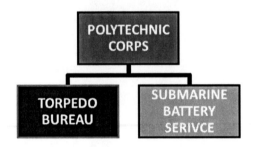

The Torpedo Bureau had a difficult mission; not only were they to keep pace with new changes in technology, but simultaneously develop innovative new technologies in the area of warfare. These SSB detachment operators needed to figure out how to take a floating explosive and turn it into a projectile, if possible, in order to hit an enemy vessel. The torpedoes of the time were mostly buoys towed behind ships to keep an enemy ship from getting too

---

[160] Craig Pippen.

[161] David Winfred Gaddy.

close, or a mine on the end of a stick; when poked it would explode.[162] R.O. Crowley was an electrician of the Torpedo Bureau, and he was part of the "research and development team". His skills were so sought after and critical to the SSB that he was given a document to have on his person at all times, it read:

"The bearer R.O. Crowley, is in the service of the Confederate States Navy as electrician; and in case of his capture by the United States forces, he will be exchanged for any general officer of their army who may be in our hands.

(Signed) S.R. Mallory
Secty. Of the Navy.

Approved.
(Signed) Jeff'N Davis, Presdt.[163]

This is a clear indication of how important Crowley was, and how critical his knowledge was to the Confederacy. He first worked with Captain Matthew Fontaine (M.F.) Maury, but he was sent to Europe to further his experiments with underwater explosives, and so his protégé, Lieutenant Hunter Davidson was to be the man to develop torpedo weaponry stateside. Davidson was born in Washington City and attended the United States Naval Academy, graduating in 1847. He served in the United States Navy from 1847 until 1861 when he

---

[162] Tom Chaffin, *The H.L. Hunley: The Secret Hope of the Confederacy*, (New York: Hill and Wang, 2008), 36.

[163] R.O. Crowley, 290.

joined the Confederate Navy. [164] These two men conducted various experiments to test hypotheses of their torpedoes *(mine was not a word used to describe underwater explosives; all were considered torpedoes during the 1860s)*.

Testing became very specific, and rightfully so, since they were dealing with explosives. During initial trial runs, they had to figure out how to keep water from reaching the interior of the boiler iron they were using as a container. It was decided to put greased cotton where the two drilled holes were located for electrical wires. These wires were designed to break, thus initiating the blasting device for the explosive. There was even a discussion regarding the container's shape. First, copper soda-water tanks were used but their buoyancy was a factor. [165] However, had they realized they were actually on to something and stuck with the copper, it's possible they may have been able to develop what today is commonly referred to as a "shape charge". A shape charge would have had even more devastating effects on Union ships; and quite possibly could have changed the outcome of the war.

Attempts at keeping the Union Navy at bay were becoming more and more difficult for the men of the Torpedo Bureau. The *"Rains Patent"* was a plan developed by the General to protect Mobile Bay in Alabama from Union war ships. All of the torpedoes used by the Confederates at Mobile were mechanical,

---

[164] "Commander Hunter Davidson, Confederate States Navy," accessed February 9, 2014, http://www.history.navy.mil/photos/pers-us/uspers-d/h-davdsn.htm.

[165] R.O. Crowley, 291.

not electric as were used in other ports. Most of these mechanical torpedoes consisted of tin cans filled with small amounts of gunpowder with a trigger mechanism attached to detonate the device. Others were made of sheet iron with a pressure switch that would set it off once contact was made by a vessel.

Another device that was designed by the Torpedo Bureau and first used in the Rains Patent was the spar torpedo. It was designed to be placed at the end of a long pole, or spar, and then attached to a boat. The weapon is used by running the spar into an enemy ship, then detonating the torpedo by use of a long chain. Spar torpedoes were often equipped with a barbed spear at the end so they would stick to wooden hulls.

Confederate Torpedo (Mine)

The device was a success and sunk the Union ironclad *Tecumseh*. [166] A spar torpedo was used by the H.L. Hunley when it made history in Charleston Harbor. The submarine was a vessel that Lieutenant H. Davidson insisted to his chain of command was needed. He understood the power of the torpedo if it had a more viable and reliable delivery system that would drive fear into the hearts of the Union sailors as they sat peacefully in Southern harbors.

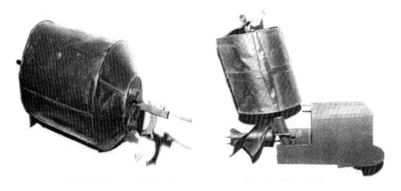

Confederate, Percussion Type Torpedoes (Mines).

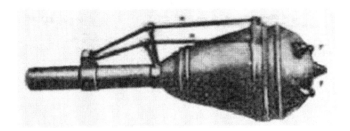

Spar torpedo used during the War of Northern Aggression.

---

[166] Ibid, 299-300.

"...Ship? Out of danger?"
– Captain Spock

Not everyone was convinced that the underwater torpedo was the answer to devastating the Union fleet. What if one could attack a ship from within without anyone onboard even knowing? Was such a covert operation possible? The answer would come in the form of Thomas Edgeworth Courtenay (*right*). Courtenay was born in Belfast, Ireland on 19 April 1822. He moved to St. Louis, MO when he was eighteen and transported goods, and especially cotton, up and down the Mississippi River where he established himself as a keen businessman. Courtenay also owned an insurance company in St. Louis, and in 1860, was elected sheriff of St. Louis County. As soon as the War Between the States broke out, Courtenay, like so many others from Missouri, sided with the Confederacy. Upon enlisting, he was given a commission as a Captain, and he sent his family to Maryland to stay with his wife's uncle.[167]

Thomas Courtney worked long and hard on a plan to destroy the naval blockade in order to reestablish Confederate shipping. There are two reasons why this was necessary. One; he was involved in the cotton industry and needed it up and running so he could continue financially, and Two; he wasn't paid a

---

[167]"Thomas Edgeworth Courtenay," accessed February 9, 2014, http://scourt.tempdomainname.com/tec.htm.

regular salary for his service. Rather, Courtenay was compensated as a privateer; receiving 50% of the value of every ship he destroyed. Therefore, the only way he could make a living was by figuring out a way to sink ships and stop the blockade. He came up with the *coal torpedo*. His invention was an iron casting of an actual piece of coal. It was then covered with beeswax, and black paint (pitch) to seal it. Lastly, it was covered with bits of actual coal to add realism. It had a threaded hole for a screw, where four ounces of gunpowder would be poured inside. In 1863, he received approval from President Jefferson Davis to enact his plan and was provided up to twenty men from the Secret Service Bureau to assist in his endeavor.[168]

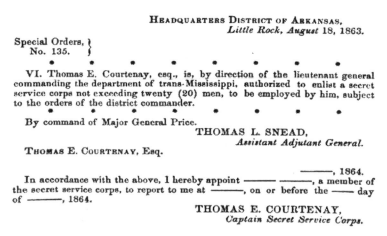

HEADQUARTERS DISTRICT OF ARKANSAS,
Little Rock, August 18, 1863.

Special Orders, ⎫
  No. 135. ⎭

*   *   *   *   *   *   *   *

VI. Thomas E. Courtenay, esq., is, by direction of the lieutenant general commanding the department of trans-Mississippi, authorized to enlist a secret service corps not exceeding twenty (20) men, to be employed by him, subject to the orders of the district commander.

*   *   *   *   *   *   *   *

By command of Major General Price.

THOMAS L. SNEAD,
Assistant Adjutant General.

THOMAS E. COURTENAY, Esq.

————, 1864.

In accordance with the above, I hereby appoint ———— ————, a member of the secret service corps, to report to me at ————, on or before the —— day of ————, 1864.

THOMAS E. COURTENAY,
Captain Secret Service Corps.

With approval from the Confederacy in hand, Courtenay set out to prove that his new invention worked. He was able to get the coal torpedoes aboard Union vessels, and now all he had to do was sit and

---

[168] Spencer C. Tucker, 391.

wait for the fireworks display. The first ship to fall victim to Courtenay's invention was the *Greyhound,* which just happened to be the command headquarters vessel for Union General Benjamin Butler. The next ship was the *USS Chenango* which exploded and sustained heavy damage while leaving New York Harbor. Thomas Courtenay proved that his invention was a success, but he wasn't the only Secret Service Bureau agent to use it. Confederate agents received word of the success that the coal torpedo was having on Union vessels. So, they came up with a plan to use it to destroy the United States Arsenal in Springfield, Massachusetts in December 1864. They placed the lump of "coal" under the major stairwell and left. The piece of "coal" was discovered by a night watchman before the fuse had time to be lit. The Canadian agents were not caught. Unfortunately, for the Union, this was not the last time the coal torpedo would be used.[169]

On 27 April, 1865, the *Sultana* was a ship carrying recently released Union POWs on its way back home when the ship exploded and sank, killing 1,700. Secret Service Bureau agent, Robert Loudon claimed to have used the coal torpedo to take the ship down in an act of defiance.[170] The Confederate government clearly stated that it was not to be used against civilian ships or ships carrying prisoners or the wounded. This was an act that the South did not need to deal with in April of 1865. The coal torpedo was an ingenious invention and a pioneering use of covert operations. Thomas Edgeworth Courtenay and

---

[169] Spencer C. Tucker, 391.

[170] Ibid.

his *infernal sabotage weapon* were way ahead of their time, as was another Confederate pioneer.

"... and the sea will grant each man new hope, as sleep brings dreams of home."
– Christopher Columbus

It has already been viewed that the Confederate States of America were well ahead in the race for inventive and new ways to conduct warfare. Southerners had no choice but to use their minds because they were, in all reality, grossly outnumbered with regards to ships, equipment and actual men on the ground fighting. Due to the realities the South was facing, a great vessel would be built and tested. The vessel was designed and built under the Submarine Battery Service of the Polytechnic Corps, and its name is the ***H.L. Hunley.*** There has been much debate about this vessel in every respect, and since her discovery in 1995 and subsequent resurrection in 2000, the debates have become even more heated.

The story begins with the need to destroy the Union blockade. It is interesting to see, how this blockade enacted by the Federals, motivated so many people to design and build new inventions of destruction. The H.L. Hunley was no exception. She would go down in history as the first submarine to actually sink an enemy vessel. The Union, in all its "hoopla" always wants to lay claim to being the first at everything during the War of Northern Aggression, and the "submarine race" was no different. It is understood that the *Alligator,* which was the Union's experimental submarine, was bound for Charleston Harbor in April of 1863. The claim is that it was the first successful submarine of the War Between the States. There is also debate that, "there was no vessel of its kind prior to this", which was April of 1863. [171] Therefore the *Hunley*, as it was to be called, would have had to been built after April of 1863. This is a false accusation because it is a proven fact that the *Hunley* conducted trial runs in July of 1863, and earlier in 1862, Hunley, McClintock and Watson had already built the *Pioneer* (another submarine), but were forced to scuttle her to prevent its capture by Union forces when New Orleans was lost. [172] Therefore, one can speculate that the Union military may have simply copied Confederate plans, stole the technology, and built a vessel naming it the *Alligator*. However, winners write history therefore I digress.

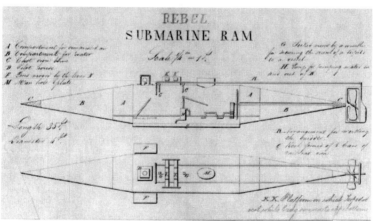

Figure 7-1. Drawing of the "Rebel Submarine Ram" in 1862.
Photo courtesy of National Archives.

---

[171] Smithsonian Channel, "America's Lost Submarine," Released 2010.

[172] "NavSource Online: Submarine Photo Archive Pioneer," accessed February 15, 2013, http://www.navsource.org/archives/08/08448.htm.

"If the only tool you have is a hammer, you tend to see every problem as a nail."
– Abraham Maslow

James McClintock *(below)* and Baxter Watson were the two mechanics that built the *Hunley*, with McClintock given credit as its chief designer. James McClintock was born and raised in Cincinnati, OH,

and left home at an early age to join a riverboat crew that navigated up and down the Mississippi river. He met Watson when they worked together as steam gauge manufacturers in New Orleans. When war broke out, McClintock and Watson set out to build a submarine but needed financial backing in order to complete their design. This is when Louisiana planter, Horace Lawson Hunley, who contributed *$30,000* towards the endeavor joined the team. [173] With his money and their design, the *"Secret Weapon of the Confederacy"* would be built. The first attempt to build the vessel was surprisingly successful, and this vessel was named the *Pioneer*. Being a two person vessel, the

---

[173] Mike Dash, "The Amazing (If True) Story of the Submarine Mechanic Who Blew Himself Up Then Surfaced as a Secret Agent for Queen Victoria. The leading mechanic of the famed H.L. Hunley led quite the life, if we can believe any of it," last modified June 30, 2014, http://www.smithsonianmag.com/history/amazing-if-true-story-submarine-mechanic-who-blew-himself-then-surfaced-secret-agent-queen-victoria-180951905/?no-ist.

Pioneer was a cigar shaped submarine that had a small conning tower for the ship's captain to peek out of (because it was so small) and control the dive plane and rudder.[174] When the vessel made its dive, however, the only air available was what it could hold within its small confines. It is estimated that would have been about 15 minutes of oxygen because there was no snorkel built into the vessel, one of its flaws.

While the Union conducted their blockade of the shipping lanes and denied use of the port, they were busy making plans to take the city of New Orleans by force. When the city fell, McClintock, Baxter and Hunley had no choice but to scuttle the *Pioneer* to prevent the vessel from falling into Union hands. With the *Pioneer* gone for good, the men moved their operation to Mobile, AL to continue the process of trial and error on the development of their revolutionary submarine.[175] The second vessel built was the *American Diver* (also known as the *Pioneer II*). This submarine was very similar to the *Pioneer*, except it could hold a crew of five, was a foot longer, and had large port holes in the conning tower for the captain of the boat to look through. Another added feature, nonexistent in the original *Pioneer*, was a compass used to navigate the vessel while traveling above the water line and when it was entirely submerged. [176]

---

[174] Chaffin, 70.

[175] Spencer C. Tucker, 915.

[176] Chaffin, 89-90.

Remembering the propulsion issues with the earlier submarine, there was an attempt by McClintock to put an electric motor inside the American Diver to turn the propeller. This proved unsuccessful because the electric engine was not able to muster enough power for the vessel. The idea of steam power was tossed into the ring, which may have worked. The problem was that the *American Diver* was already in the final stages of production and would not be able to hold a steam engine within her bowels.[177] Once again, the hand crank method would have to be the propulsion method of choice.

The trial runs of the American Diver were subpar. The ship was never able to go over two miles per hour with the crew cranking with all their might. This made the vessel inferior, and it sealed her fate in early 1863 when the boat sunk into Mobile Bay.[178] This had to be disheartening for the builders, designer and the financial backer since two vessels had been lost in less than a year. The team was going to give it one more go, and this third vessel would prove to be the one that would make history.

"But who shall tell us now what sort of Navy to build?"
– President Woodrow Wilson

The three men were at it again, attempting to build a submersible ship that would bring the might of the Union Navy to its knees. This ship was to be named the *CSS H.L. Hunley* in honor of its primary

---

[177] Chaffin, 91-92.

[178] Ibid, 97.

investor who had stuck with the program for the entire duration. This ship was built in Mobile, AL just as the *American Diver* was, and later moved to Charleston, SC by rail on 12 August 1863 following its successful trial runs. Once it arrived there the Confederate military took control of the vessel and put it under the control of General P.T. Beauregard, the garrison commander and defender of Charleston.[179] The first crew readied themselves for a night mission to attack a Union blockade ship in the harbor on 29 August 1863. Under the command of Lieutenant John A. Payne, the crew set out on their voyage to make history. However, that was not to be the case. It wasn't long after leaving port, when the ship disappeared suddenly. There was a crew of nine on board, and five of them went down with the ship:

Michael Cane
Nicholas Davis
Frank Doyle
John Kelly
Absolum Williams

Charles Hasker, one of the surviving crewmembers recalled that, *"John A. Payne, accidentally stepped on the lever controlling the dive planes causing the submarine to dive while her hatches were still open."* [180] The vessel was recovered as quickly as possible and a second crew assembled.

---

[179] "H.L. Hunley," accessed March 5, 2013,
http://www.sonofthesouth.net/leefoundation/h-l-hunley-submarine.htm.

[180] "Friends of the Hunley First Crew," accessed March 5, 2013,
http://hunley.org/main_index.asp?CONTENT=FIRSTCREW.

Chapter 7 Polytechnic Corps

On 15 October, 1863, the *Hunley* had onboard, crew No.2 consisting of:

> *Horace Hunley – Captain*
> *Robert Brookbank,*
> *Joseph Patterson,*
> *Thomas W. Park*
> *Charles McHugh,*
> *Henry Baird*
> *John Marshall*
> *Charles L. Sprague*

Not one man would make it back to the shore of South Carolina alive. All went down with the mighty ship to include her namesake and financial backer, Horace Lawson Hunley. The following is the explanation of what happened to Crew No. 2:

"If the crew had been able to close the forward sea valve, the freezing water that had already entered the ballast tank and spilled over the top could have been bailed back into the compartment and pumped into the sea. In the darkness and confusion that followed the impact with the ocean floor, the valve handle must have fallen off the stem and become lost beneath the bodies that had been thrown into the forward area. As icy water and internal pressure steadily rose within the vessel, panic would have gripped the terrified crewmen. Beneath nine fathoms, hopelessly stuck in the mud, their shouts for help were soon silenced by the biting cold water at the black bottom of Charleston Harbor."[181]

---

[181] "Friends of the Hunley First Crew," accessed March 5, 2013, http://hunley.org/main_index.asp?CONTENT=SECONDCREW.

The last and final crew No.3, were the ones to make history, but never afforded the opportunity to bask in the glory. This final crew was:

Lieutenant George E. Dixon *(Northerner)*
Joseph Ridgaway *(Maryland)* 2-IC
Arnold Becker *(European)*
Corporal J. F. Carlsen *(European)*
Frank Collins *(Virginia)*
Augustus Miller *(European)*
James A. Wicks *(North Carolina)*[182]

It is known that the ship left the harbor on the night of 17 February 1864, to attack a Union blockade ship, the *USS Housatonic.* The Hunley had on her bow a spar torpedo with 90 pounds of explosive contained within. Finding the *Housatonic,* the *Hunley* rammed into her, driving her explosive payload into the side of the Union vessel and backed away. The *Housatonic* exploded and sunk to the ocean depths. However, after making her kill, the *Hunley* never returned to shore. Her entire crew went down with her; lost until she was discovered in the mid-90's. There has always been a great deal of speculation as to what caused the *Hunley* to sink. Some of the hypotheses; the crew was too close to the blast and was knocked unconscious, suffocating without knowing it, or she was hit by a naval gun round and this caused her to sink.

A test was conducted in a ballistics lab that put an end, hopefully, to the assumptions of what took down the *Hunley.* From evidence found on the ship in connection with leading historians, ballistic experts, and archeologists, the team's conclusion

---

[182] Secret Weapon of the Confederacy: National Geographic.

was that the *Hunley* sank when her port hole was shot by a sailor aboard the *Housatonic* when the vessel was spotted right before she set her charge. Either the *Hunley* dove to escape any further onslaught or the turbulent water filled the ship and she sank with her last and final crew.[183] Although she never returned to port, the *H.L. Hunley* made history as the first submarine to conduct a combat mission to sink an enemy vessel during a time of war.

The innovators of the Polytechnic Corps of the Confederate Secret Service Bureau changed the way modern warfare is fought, even to this day. The designer and builders of the *Hunley*, as well as the designer of the coal torpedo, all were thinking about new ways to defeat an enemy other than large "conventional" land battles. These men forever changed how countries conduct war, and how they assess enemy capability. No longer were large units or forces required to make huge impacts during times of war or conflict.

---

[183] Secret Weapon of the Confederacy: National Geographic.

USS Housatonic. First ship to be sunk by a submarine.

CSS Hunley with its bow-mounted spar torpedo. Courtesy Dan Dowdy.

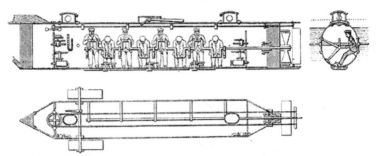

Photo # NH 58769 Cutaway drawings of the Confederate submarine H.L. Hunley

FIG. 175 à 177. — Le *David* de Hunley reconstitué d'après les dessins de M. William-A. Alexander (1863).

CSS Hunley cutaway. Courtesy US Navy.

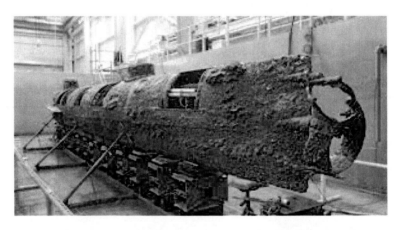

CSS Hunley in the preservation tank in Charleston, SC

"Consider the subtleness of the sea; how it's most dreaded creatures glide under water, unapparent for the most part, and treacherously hidden beneath the loveliest tints of azure."
– Melville, Moby-Dick

Chapter 8

Splinter Detachments and Bureaus

"A serious prophet upon predicting a flood should be the first man to climb a tree. This would demonstrate that he was indeed a seer."
– Stephen Crane

As one can see, there were a great deal of other organizations that were part of the Confederate Secret Service Bureau and Signal Corps. Most of these bodies operated as independent entities that were created out of necessity. Often times, once a bureaucrat or general officer in Richmond discovered what a particular organization was doing through the 'good ol' boy system, they'd finagle the command of the organization, therefore able to better direct its activities and take credit for its successes. When a need was discovered that wasn't readily found in the private sector, the government was forced to create it from scratch. Here is a small list of some of the other bureaus or detachments that were within the Confederate War Department that systematically supported the Secret Service Bureau and Signal Corps. Almost a *Group Support Battalion*, of modern Special Operations Units:

Commissary and Quarter Master Bureau
Conscript Bureau
Construction Bureau
Ordnance and Hydrography Bureau
Engineer Bureau

Indian Affairs Bureau
Foreign Affairs Bureau
Provost Marshal of Richmond
Prison Camp Bureau
Prisoner Exchange Bureau
Niter and Mining Bureau
Company A, Secret Service Detachment
Lighthouse Bureau
Post office Appointment and Contract Bureau
War Tax Bureau
Produce Loan Bureau
War Bureau
Strategic Bureau
Strategy Bureau

Not all of the above listed bureaus had a direct impact on the SSB with regards to support. Some of the bureaus did their own thing during the war, never realizing the SSB existed or that they provided indirect support. However, a select few bureaus understood they supported the SSB and knew exactly what their involvement entailed.

> ***"What one man can invent another can discover."***
> – *Sherlock Holmes*

Though agents were already conducting sabotage and subversion operations out of Canada, the Confederate Secret Service Bureau wanted a group of "local" agents that weren't "commissioners" appointed by President Davis. This detachment became *Company A, of the Confederate Secret Service.*[184] The authorization for this unit came by

---

[184] Tidwell, *April '65*, 51.

way of a resolution proposed by Louisiana Senator Edward Sparrow before the Confederate Senate on 20 January, 1864, to "officially" form the "secret company". The resolution passed the Senate and the House without difficulty. According to an amendment attached to the resolution, the men of *Company A* would work without salary, instead receiving a commission based on a calculation of 4% of whatever they destroyed. On 22 January, President Davis signed the resolution and on 4 February, 1864, Zere McDaniel received a letter from the Confederate Secretary of War James A. Seddon, *"to raise a company of no more than 50 men...and report to Brigadier General Gabriel Rains"*.[185]

It was neither by accident, nor political favor that Zere McDaniel was commissioned as a captain in the Confederate Army in 1863, and later selected to lead this new and innovative detachment. [186] McDaniel had already amassed a lengthy resume of experience in subversion and sabotage. He was also no stranger to General Rains; having previously worked for him in the Torpedo Bureau. One of McDaniel's many accomplishments during the war occurred two years earlier.

The *USS Cairo* was the lead ship of the *City-class* ironclad river gunboats built at Mound City, Illinois, and was a member of the U.S. Army's Western Gunboat Flotilla in 1862. This ship was involved in many engagements in Tennessee, and operated on the Mississippi and Ohio Rivers and their tributaries. She was quite the site having thirteen large guns on

---

[185] "Spies and Conspiracy," accessed June 12, 2014, http://www.ourarchives.wikispaces.net/Spies+and+Conspiracy.

[186] "Spies and Conspiracy."

her deck.[187] The *USS Cairo* (below) was viewed as a formidable object that needed to be taken out to ensure freedom of maneuver for the Confederate military forces operating in the west.

On 12 December 1862, *Operation Yazoo* was well underway in an attempt to destroy Union vessels, or at a minimum, restrict their movement on the river.[188] Zere McDaniel and another member of his detachment, Francis M. Ewing, were setting torpedoes in the Yazoo River, approximately seven miles north of Vicksburg, MS. They built their destructive devices in a small building within the wood line just off the banks of the river. Their

---

[187] "Online Library of Selected Images: U.S. Navy Ships, USS Cairo," accessed September 21, 2013, http://www.history.navy.mil/photos/sh-usn/usnsh-c/cairo.htm.

[188] "USS Cairo Gunboat and Museum," accessed December 21, 2013, http://www.nps.gov/vick/u-s-s-cairo-gunboat.htm.

torpedo of choice for this operation were a pair of demijohns. McDaniel believed, through his experiments, that it was vital to have the torpedo go off very close to or in contact with the target vessel's hull, so he built his torpedoes in pairs, with a line between them, tied to the loops of the friction primers; the idea being that the boat would hit the line and bring both torpedoes up against her sides, and the jolt would set them off. A single demijohn consisted of a five gallon container full of black powder utilizing a friction primer.

Friction primers were in common use in both armies and navies by the end of 1862. Simply constructed, they were "a copper tube filled with powder; at the top of the tube was soldered a short tube containing a compound of antimony sulphide and potassium chlorate; lying in that composition was a roughened wire; the other end of the wire was twisted into a loop so that a lanyard could be hooked to it."[189] They were compact, easy to use, and more moisture-resistant than the older percussion cap method of firing artillery; a hard tug on the lanyard pulled the "roughened" wire through the explosive chemical composition in the primer. The most important advantage of the friction primer was, that in the backwoods of Mississippi, McDaniel didn't have much access to electrical equipment; but he was able to beg or borrow primers from artillery units in order to alter for his own purposes.

Just as McDaniel had planned it, when the flotilla of Union river boats were making their way around the sharp bend on the Yazoo River, they came under harassing fire by fellow Confederates. This was an

---

[189] John C. Wideman, *The Sinking of the USS Cairo,* (Jackson, MS, University Press of Mississippi, 2004), 17.

almost perfectly set up, textbook ambush. The *USS Cairo* was in the back of the pack, but moved up to assist the smaller, less protected boats that had been sent forward to clear Confederate torpedoes. As she made her way to the front, the *Cairo* hit the lanyard, pulling both torpedoes up along the sides of her hull, setting off the daisy chained torpedoes. It threw the ship in the air with her thirteen guns being thrown from the ship. The vessel was totally destroyed and sank to a depth of thirty-six feet under water in less than ten minutes. However, to the surprise of both parties, no one was killed. [190] The *USS Cairo* was salvaged in the 1960's and is now on display at the National Battlefield Park in Vicksburg, MS undergoing reconstruction and restoration.

Besides riverine improvised explosive devices (IEDs), McDaniel was an expert with various types of land torpedoes as well; skills he would soon share with his new team of *Company A* saboteurs.

Sycamore Row, Buffalo Lithia Springs, Va.

Located in south central Virginia, not far from, and therefore, safely within the defenses of Richmond, existed a popular resort known as Buffalo Springs. The resort (left) was first established in the 18th century and could easily accommodate hundreds of guests. During the War of Northern Aggression, the Confederacy selected

---

[190] Gabriel J. Rains and Peter S. Michie, *Confederate Torpedoes: Two Illustrated 19th Century Works with New Appendices and Photographs,* (Jefferson, NC: McFarland, 2011), 140-141.

Buffalo Springs to serve as its *Irregular Warfare Operations School*. The four-week long course taught the Secret Service recruits all they needed to know in order to be able to conduct covert and clandestine operations.[191] Needless to say, had they not been successful conducting covert operations during the war, assuredly more people would be "talking" about them today.

Company A turned out to be a huge success under McDaniel's leadership, and no doubt the forerunner to the Jedburgh teams of World War II. *Company A* operated in a similar fashion as the Jedburghs, though eighty years earlier. (*The mission of the Jedburgh teams was to "supplement existing SO/SOE circuits, procure intelligence ...and to take part in sabotage operations."*). [192] The missions these men conducted behind enemy lines were not spoken of, or written about. The clandestine nature of their activities lacked the flamboyancy one generally expects from a Southern gentleman of the 1860s; which is why most of their adventures have alluded historians to this day. These guys were far from flamboyant; they were the true *Special Forces Operators* or *Jedburghs* (*Jeds*) of the South.

One mission conducted by *Company A* seems as though it comes right out of a covert action thriller movie. *Operation City Point* was a covert action that again was to be conducted by an operational two man team. The target given to the team by Captain McDaniel was City Point, VA and the Union supply

---

[191] Tidwell, *April '65*, 97-98.

[192] "Jedburghs," accessed December 14, 2013, http://www.soc.mil/OSS/jedburghs.html.

depot located there. The two men chosen for the mission were John A. Maxwell and R.K. Dillard. They conducted a thorough reconnaissance of the target area in order to determine what, when and how best to attack the site. Based on their reconnaissance, the two men decided to use what they called a *horological bomb*, or commonly referred to as a time bomb. This devise consisted of twelve pounds of explosives in a sealed container or box, a timekeeping device, and a primer to initiate the charge.[193]

Just before sunrise on 9 August, 1864, the men moved up to the supply depot. Maxwell went forward and Dillard stayed behind. It is said that Dillard was the better of the two at sabotage; but common sense would say that he was there to provide over watch in case things did not go as planned. Maxwell observed the captain of a barge disembark his vessel and move out of the line of sight of the ship. This was the time for him to make his move. Walking up to the sentry, who was a German immigrant that did not speak English well at all, Maxwell was immediately challenged by the sentry. Maxwell, being the cool and calm saboteur, informed the sentry that he had orders to put the box on the ship by the captain. With the sentry temporarily confused, Maxwell called for a worker from the deck of the ship to assist him with loading the "package".

Handing the oblivious deck hand the box, Maxwell made his way out of the area. Maxwell and Dillard set up an observation site not too far from the supply depot so they could witness the explosion. When the hand on the clock face struck 11:30 a.m., the primer struck and so did the charge. The explosion was

---

[193] Wideman, 69.

monumental! The men were utterly surprised at how destructive a mere twelve pounds of explosives could be; and being so close, Dillard was temporarily rendered deaf. What they didn't know at the time was the barge they had chosen was a magazine ship. It contained within her, *"100 boxes of artillery projectiles, 2,000 boxes of small arms ammunition, 600-700 blank rounds, and 1 keg of mortar powder."*[194]

The total casualties that the Union suffered were; 43 dead, 126 wounded, $2 million dollars' worth of military storage, equipment, vessels, armament, the ordnance boat *Kendrick,* and the barge *General Mede.*[195]

City Point, Virginia after the explosion. Courtesy of National Archives, Records of the Office of the Chief Signal Officer.

---

[194] Wideman, 70.

[195] Ibid, 70.

The similarities between *Company A* and the Office of Strategic Services (OSS) that operated during WWII are too similar to be coincidental. Both consisted of specialized small teams that conducted espionage, subversion, and sabotage behind enemy lines. *Company A,* much like the OSS eighty years later, had a school that trained their operators to prepare them for what they were expected to do, and had a selection process to ensure only the best joined their ranks. And also like the OSS, *Company A* had a fearless and competent leader in Zere McDaniel; a charismatic officer that led by example and was a specialized and skilled covert operator.

Company A would not be remembered amongst the more celebrated units such as Lee's Army of Northern Virginia, or Mosby's 43rd "Ranger" Battalion, but they were a formidable fighting force and a specialized detachment of the much larger Confederate Secret Service.

A torpedo designed by Zere McDaniel that was discovered during the capture of Richmond. It is housed at the United States Military Academy Museum. Courtesy US Military Academy.

"A traitor is everyone who does not agree with me."
– *King George III*

Brigadier General John H. Winder (below), of Maryland was a former instructor at West Point, and was one of President Jefferson Davis' instructors. There is speculation, that is why Jefferson appointed him Provost of the Army of the Confederate States effective 21 June, 1861. [196] His main duties and responsibilities are vague at best. It is known though that he was in charge of Union prisoners, military order and discipline within the limits of Richmond, the defenses of Richmond, and counterespionage.[197]

However, Winder went pretty much ballistic with his duties of Richmond; one could call it a *"power trip"*. He decided to ban the sale of any liquor within the confines of the city, and all privately owned firearms had to be surrendered to the Confederate Ordnance Bureau. Additionally, at any given time, all hotels and passenger systems had to provide a detailed list

---

[196] Tidwell, *April '65*, 45.

[197] Ibid, 45.

of people's coming and going in and out of the city. And lastly, he insisted on the issuance of a passport to leave the city. [198] There was more than what is listed, but these were by far the worst. He also hired most of the members of his counter espionage team from Baltimore, Maryland. [199] Maryland, if you remember, even though being a Northern state, had Southern sympathies. One such individual was Major Norris; a Marylander and Southerner at heart. Norris wasn't as zealous as Winder. However, he was responsible for confining thirty suspected Union sympathizers to prison in Richmond,[200] though the act itself may have been nothing more than an elaborate cover up.

Elizabeth Van Lew aka *"Crazy Bet"* was a Union spy that had developed her own network within Richmond. She had access to the highest levels of the government and collected vital intelligence that was instrumental to the war against the Confederacy. Elizabeth or *Lizzie* was a Southerner with Northern sympathies. Like some Southerners, she attested the thought of slavery and wanted it abolished. Although she was not as vocal as her thoughts were, she did so under a cloak of darkness. Libby Prison in Richmond was full of Union soldiers (prisoners of war). She was able to get a pass to visit these Union soldiers along with her mother in order to provide the prisoners bare necessities, as well as

---

[198] Thomas, 151.

[199] Tidwell, April '65, 46.

[200] Thomas, 151.

limited medical care whenever a Confederate doctor could be persuaded to accompany her.[201]

She began collecting intelligence from the incarcerated soldiers and passing it off to Union operatives within the city of Richmond. As time wore on, she had to devise even cleverer methods of passing information back and forth. She hid messages in medicine bottles, developed a bowl that contained a false bottom to conceal a message, and books that would have pin pricks from a needle to send the message. When the guards suspected her of being up to no good, she began to not care for herself any longer as a ploy. She would not bathe nor brush her hair, and was given the nickname *Crazy Bet* by the locals.

On one occasion her prison pass was revoked. Upset, she went to see an old family friend, *Brigadier General John H. Winder, the Provost Marshall of Richmond,* who scolded her for having it revoked and issued her a new one. Not only that, but one of her former slaves she had freed, somehow made it into Richmond, and became part of her spy ring, and even received a job working for President Jefferson Davis at his residence.[202]

How was it, General Winder was unable to capture, apprehend, and crush an active spy ring operating within his own city? Was the Provost Marshall actually working for the Union? There is no other logical explanation. Some have said that he was overwhelmed with his duties; and that sounds

---

[201] Tom Moon, *Loyal and Lethal Ladies of Espionage,* (Bloomington, IN: iUniverse, 2000), 14-15.

[202] Moon, 17.

like an excuse because the man had more than enough people under his command. To be exact, a total of *forty-six, with nine in his (personal) office, six at Castle Thunder (prison) including three detectives, and thirty-one in the provost marshal's office including thirteen detectives"*.[203]

In 1864, one year before Richmond was captured by Union troops, his staff suddenly became more concerned with counterespionage than with other matters of the city.[204] Now, this could be attributed to the numerous battles that occurred that year: Fort Fisher, Cold Harbor, Meridian, Wilderness, Spotsylvania Courthouse, Yellow Tavern, Crater at Petersburg, Kennesaw Mountain, Monocay, Tupelo, Cedar Creek, and Nashville. Not to mention the fact that General Grant in the same year had been given command of the entire army. Further, "somehow" 109 Union soldiers were able to escape from Libby Prison in Richmond, with 59 making it to Union lines.[205] Even Allen Dulles, first civilian director of the Central Intelligence Agency and former OSS operative, commented on the carelessness of Winder,

"His own slapdash to security rivaled that of his careless Union counterparts. He kept a blackboard in his office so he could retrieve information easily. Among the items chalked on his board was a complete list of the regiments defending the Confederate

---

[203] Tidwell, April '65, 46.

[204] Ibid, 46-47.

[205] "Civil War Timeline," accessed December 21, 2014, http://www.nps.gov/gett/historyculture/civil-war-timeline.htm.

capital, which were left in plain sight for any visitor to jot down and pass to Union spies."[206]

This is no coincidence; the war for the Confederacy was beginning to look bleak with the loss of the *H.L. Hunley, CSS Alabama,* and the death of J.E.B. Stuart. All the facts and information point to Winder, most likely, serving as an intelligence officer for the Union; a decision that appears to be motivated by his former loyalties, such as being an instructor at West Point, and driven by discontent on being given such a medial position within the Confederate military.

> **"Well, all day long at school I hear how great Marcia is at this or how wonderful Marcia did that! Marcia, Marcia, Marcia!"**
> *– Jan Brady*

The realization by the Confederate government that a need existed for a specialized unit of saboteurs that could operate behind enemy lines didn't occur overnight by epiphany. Prior to the establishment of *Company A,* there were several splinter detachments of larger organizations doing their very best at conducting these specialized missions in an effort to stop the Union invader. The *Engineer Bureau* was one such organization. After all, it only made sense at the time to use engineers to perform "destructionist actions".

Bernard Janin Sage was a big advocate of the Engineer Bureau receiving a detachment of destructionists to carry out clandestine operations

---

[206] Michael J. Sulick, *Spying In America: Espionage from the Revolutionary War to the Dawn of 66.*

under the command of the respective theatre commanders.[207] However, it didn't take long before the flaw of this thinking became readily apparent to the leadership in Richmond.

There were several lessons learned from these earlier experiments with conducting sabotage. One was the officers of a conventional engineer unit struggled to provide coherent orders to their detachment of destructionists to conduct clandestine operations. Another was that the destructionists, themselves, were inadequately trained and generally unprepared for the very missions they were assigned to conduct. Another fatal flaw of this plan was the destructionists from the *Engineer Bureau* would be co-located wherever the mass of the military might was at that time, near or within earshot of the front lines. There was no true way for these guys to be able to stealthily move in and out of an area, as the detachment members of *Company A,* later, could and did on a regular basis.

Bernard Sage first called the detachment of "destructionists" under the Engineer Bureau the "Organization of Private Warfare".[208] He was doing everything in his power to get the approval through the Confederate House and Senate to begin conducting operations. The act was finally approved on 19 March, 1863, and the men chosen for the task(s) were to report to the area of operation they wished to serve in, enlist, and be organized as an engineer company.[209]

---

[207] Tidwell, April '65, 106.

[208] Ibid, 98.

[209] Ibid, 99.

However, the plan was for these men to be able to operate independently within the engineer company, not members of said organization. Sage sent a copy of a pamphlet he created to General Rains on his proposal and waited for a reply. Rains expressed his approval in a unit that handled inventions systematically, and that the bureau Sage was attempting to create, should change its name to be called the *Bureau of Strategy*.[210] Rains was already at the forefront and well underway in developing and fine tuning an operational capability within his Torpedo Bureau consisting of individuals with specialized skills to perform the much needed sabotage missions. An Engineer Bureau officer by the name of Lieutenant Colonel J.A. Williams wrote to a colleague, *"Can you raise some men to bring down eight torpedoes via Drewry's Bluff? I can detail a few men here. I want them assigned for floating down upon the monitors that are shelling us. McDaniel has disappointed me."*[211] It was during this time that Zere McDaniel was working for Rain's *Torpedo Bureau.*

The "destructionists" within the Engineer Bureau were formally created, though their use appears to have been limited, as there are no solid accounts of their successes as with the unit that would take over this mission, *Company A.* It took trial and error, and valuable time for the leadership in Richmond to finally realize the organizational deficiencies of having the Engineer Bureau play in the clandestine world.

---

[210] Tidwell, April '65, 102.

[211] Wideman, 67.

"Uh, we had a slight weapons malfunction, but uh...everything's perfectly all right now. We're fine. We're all fine here now, thank you. How are you?" – Han Solo

The most important bureau that was needed for any of these clandestine organizations to run, and for that matter the Secret Navy, Secret Service Bureau, and Special and Detached Services and Signal Corps was the Ordnance and Hydrography Bureau (OHB); which was ran by Josiah Gorgas. This bureau was not directly involved in any "secret dealings" as others were, but without this bureau there would have been no sinking of the *USS Cairo*, etc. This bureau originally fell under the command of the Confederate Navy; producing uniforms, wagons, guns, pistols, sabers, shells, powder, blankets, and even casting its own naval guns.

Within two years, a sub-detachment within the OHB, the Nitre and Mining Bureau, broke away to conduct its own program of refining military minerals such as coal, iron, copper, nitre, and lead.[212] They also contracted private citizens to help with the manufacturing of goods to stimulate the economy. This bureau was so important to the war effort and clandestine operations that it was infiltrated by a Union spy in Richmond (no surprise there). He was an Austrian by birth and his name was Orazio Lugo de Antonzini, aka Doctor Lugo. Yes, another doctor to deal with in the clandestine realm. He was claiming to be a "visitor" but had on him maps,

---

[212] Thomas, 207-211.

plans, and other items of a sensitive nature. [213] Another Winder – oops.

The different detachments and bureaus of the Confederate War Department each had their own mission set. Those that supported each other had great success, while others simply looked the other way when things went array. President Jefferson Davis did his best to appoint members of his staff and cabinet that he thought best fit the bill, or politically, were in his best interest. Not once though, did he undermine the laws established or ruled upon by the Confederate government. He never took action into his own hands, instead relied heavily on his clandestine operations units to perform the duties they were assigned to do, entrusting them to do so: The character of a true leader.

Capital Building, Confederate States of America, Richmond VA ca. 1861.

---

[213] Tidwell, Come Retribution, 127.

Chapter 9
I am the Senate

"Its treason, then..."
– Supreme Chancellor Palpatine

It has long been a dream, or desire for "Civil War" historians and authors to link the Confederate government to the assassination of Union President Abraham Lincoln. Volumes upon volumes of manuscripts, photographs, and testimonies have been read through and surmised. Skeptics say it was a plan, devised from the beginning, by Jefferson Davis and his War Department. They claim the South's motive for assassinating President Lincoln was to cause disturbance and confusion throughout the North. Whereas, the plan *Come Retribution* is common knowledge for any Civil War enthusiast, historian or scholar. Interestingly enough, *Come Retribution* has not of yet been referred to as a military operation. Now why is that? An operation by definition is, *"A military action or the carrying out of a strategic, operational, tactical, service, training, or administrative military mission."*[214]

Therefore, it should be called, **Operation Come Retribution**, should it not? The story of how President Lincoln was shot by John Wilkes Booth at Ford's Theatre in Washington City is still being taught today to American school children. The people at Ford's Theatre, that were behind the scenes, like the ventriloquist with a dummy, are never connected to Booth directly or indirectly. Many were members

---

[214] FM 1-02 p 1-136.

of the Confederate Secret Service Bureau and Special and Detached Services and Signal Corps. Many have already been discussed, and the players have been placed on the field of play.

"It's an ill wind that blows no good."
– John Heywood

There was a deep distaste for President Lincoln by Southern sympathizers, and this was a key motivating factor. These people had the drive and determination, but how to actually accomplish it was another matter. There are still those out there that refuse to acknowledge the existence of any Confederate clandestine operational unit because it would ruin their "fantasy" that John Wilkes Booth planned this entire operation on his own, and carried it out so well even with the all issues that arose. Well, hate to burst any bubbles of the Civil War "buffs" out there, but John Wilkes Booth took an operation that was already planned and tweaked it to fit his objective. The assassination of President Abraham Lincoln, a pestilence as Booth viewed him, had to be removed in his mind for the Southern States to be rid of the "Yankee invaders".

First, let's look at one of the characters in this Shakespearian play, James W. Pumphrey. It is common knowledge that he was the livery or stable owner who provided Booth his horse. Pumphrey was born on 12 September, 1832, and died on 16 March, 1906. He lived an awkward life having never officially married. None the less, he had seven children from two different women. The following is written about him in the Official Pumphrey Family History Book, which is never mentioned in any historical text when referring to Pumphrey.

"James W. Pumphrey is a minor footnote in history as he was the owner and proprietor of the stable from which John Wilkes Booth rented his getaway horse when he assassinated President Abraham Lincoln. After the death of his father Levi in 1858, James inherited the livery stable at the corner of C and 6th Streets NW. The following descriptions of the events, and connection of Booth to James W. Pumphrey, are from an issue of the family newsletter of which I was editor at the time.

Even though Lee did not surrender to Grant at Appomattox courthouse until April 9, for all intents and purposes the Civil War was finished. One must now try to envision the prevalent attitude of paranoia that existed in the nation's capital in early 1865. The two main functions of the federal government were killing the Confederacy and keeping Lincoln alive.

John Wilkes Booth probably first thought of killing Lincoln in the fall of 1864, although he did not bring the other 6 conspirators into his plot until January 1865. Dr. Samuel Mudd is being excluded as a conspirator in accordance with more recent findings. Wilkes Booth and his band of 6 were in a strange amalgam of incompetent and malcontents.

Booth was vastly superior to the others in native intelligence but his egomania certainly interfered with his powers of rational thought. In any case, Booth decided to strike at Ford's theatre on April 14 and in planning his getaway he visited James W. Pumphrey's livery stable at noon on the 14th in order to arrange the rental of a horse. He told Pumphrey to have a certain roan mare saddled and ready for him at four o'clock. Always being prompt, Booth returned to the stable at precisely four and picked up the horse. He then took the mare to a small stable at the rear of Ford's theatre where he tethered her. The rest of the events at Ford's theatre that evening are known and well documented.

Although Booth was eventually killed while being captured, the other 6 conspirators were placed on trial and convicted; four of them were hanged and the other two received life sentences. At the conspiracy trial, James W. Pumphrey testified as a witness for the prosecution that John Wilkes Booth rented the horse from his livery stable the afternoon that Lincoln was shot. Pumphrey also stated that Booth had rented horses from him on several occasions during the previous 6 weeks.

James Pumphrey continued to operate his livery stable until sometime after 1900. The stable's demise (like many others) was caused by the advent of the automobile shortly after the turn of the century."[215]

There is not one history book out there with this information in it. One of his relatives copied this information from the family book, so that it could be documented elsewhere. That was the family's take on

---

[215] The Pumphrey Family Book, The Pumphrey Press, Vol. 2, No. 2, July 1980.

-I have yet to find another book on this subject that directly references the Pumphrey Family Book. Luckily, I had access to the pages that mentioned James, and his direct descendent that possessed the book told of family reunions where James was the topic of discussion. It is a travesty that this information is left out of modern books and documentaries that tell how his life was affected by the Lincoln death. This is why James is mentioned to bring to light who the man was and how he and his family dealt with their name being tarnished.

what James W. Pumphrey was involved in. What was left out was how nearly all his children lived horrible lives; either dying at a young age, or turning to prostitution. All of which had to be directly related to the role their father played. One has to remember that Pumphrey was a Southern sympathizer.[216]

James Pumphrey had known John Surratt for years because they both lived in Washington City, and based on their professions probably sent customers to each other's establishments. Surratt also introduced Pumphrey to Booth, on account that Pumphrey vows that he just doesn't rent to anyone, so that he may vouch for him so he may rent a horse. [217] Does this incriminate Pumphrey just for knowing a guy? Not as of yet, but logically one could suspect that Pumphrey was a member of the Confederate Secret Service Bureau operating in Washington City. His livery is the perfect place for operatives to rest or receive horses while staying at the Surratt Boarding house.

When Pumphrey informs Booth that he needs a recommendation, and it comes from Surratt[218], this was not a real *"recommendation"* but a challenge and password. Pumphrey was well aware that he resided in the heart of the Union, and to be asked a certain question implies he needed confirmation of what this

---

[216] Bill O'Reilly and Dwight Jon Zimmerman, *Lincoln's Last Days: The Shocking Assassination That Changed America Forever*, (New York: Square Fish, 2014), 70.

[217] Michael W. Kauffman, *John Wilkes Booth and the Lincoln Conspiracies,* (New York: Random House, 2004), 176.

[218] Ibid.

man's (Booth's) intentions were to ensure that he wasn't one of Pinkerton's boys. He received the *"recommendation"* from Surratt who was a Canadian Bureau Agent, a courier to be exact.[219]

Was it just a coincidence that a courier of the Confederate Canadian Bureau is friends with a livery stable owner who just so happens to also be a Southern sympathizer? Could it be that the livery stable owner was completely oblivious to what Booth and Surratt were up to, as well as the organizations they were members of? This is too good to be true. How can one argue, with so much circumstantial evidence, that Pumphrey was not involved with the Confederate Secret Service Bureau?

> *"The Gunpowder Treason and plot;*
> *I see of no reason why Gunpowder Treason*
> *should ever be forgot."*
> – *Guy Fawkes*

There was a man that was viewed negatively within the Union because he introduced a new method of warfare, and perhaps was also an "underground" conspirator. And why not? He had already tried once to end the life of President Lincoln. Before this man is moved to the guillotine, let's take a look at the facts surrounding Doctor Luke Pryor Blackburn and his association with John Wilkes Booth. There is testimony that was given in a secret session, not to the general public, concerning the yellow fever plot. It was said that Doctor Blackburn was in Booth's company on at least one occasion in Montreal; and that President Jefferson Davis was a member of the plot(s) with Booth and others.

---

[219] Mayers, 161.

However, this testimony was thrown out because the judges were informed that the witness had been paid by the Justice Department to provide erroneous evidence that would put Jefferson Davis in a hangman's noose.[220]

It's simply amazing how far the Union was willing to go in their attempt to pin the assassination of Lincoln on Jefferson Davis. They were so set in their mission that they even paid off a witness just to say that Davis was a member of the plot(s); and because of this, the information about Doctor Blackburn and his relations with John Wilkes Booth was thrown out. Could the doctor have been a "backer" for Booth? Did he even meet with Booth? To say that he never met with Booth would be an understatement. It is known that Booth, *"worked as a Confederate secret agent. He met frequently with the heads of the Secret Service, Jacob Thompson and Clement Clay, in Montreal."*[221]

So let's look at this again. Could the doctor have come across the path of John Wilkes Booth while in Montreal or any other meeting place or safe house in Canada? The answer is surely yes, but the question at hand is did Doctor Blackburn *(right)* have anything to do with the conspiracy to kill the President of the United States? Again, the question is

---

[220] Baird, 32.

[221] Doug Linder.

why wouldn't he have been, or more importantly, why would he have been? The man already attempted to kill the president once via biological warfare, so what would stop him from using a lead bullet with the help of some gun powder? It was clearly an attempt to take off the top tier of the enemy government; a plot that *should ever be forgot.*

"The people would be just as noisy if they were going to see me hanged."
– Oliver Cromwell

Secretary of War Edwin McMasters Stanton is said to have been cleared of any conspiracy or alleged activity concerning the assassination of President Lincoln. Yet, we know that he was a member of the Knights of the Golden Circle, a pro-South organization. We also know he was one of its top members. There is speculation, and justifiably so, that perhaps, just perhaps Stanton was an agent of the Confederate Secret Service and Signal Corps.[222] Before we dismiss the speculation, let's take a good look at the facts as they present themselves, and concede that the allegation is nothing new.

General Grant was supposed to attend the play that night with Lincoln, but was told not to go. If he had attended, not only would the opera box, but the hallway and stair case would have been littered with Union officers and guardsmen with weapons. It would have been nearly impossible for an assassin to reach the President's box. Moreover, President Lincoln's body guard was told not to go to the play because there was other pressing business that

---

[222] America Unearthed Season 2 Episode 12.

required his attention.[223] This left President Lincoln open to an attack as soon as the protective measures were removed.

Let's focus our attention to the trials. First off, the trials were conducted by a military tribunal, not a civilian court, which occurred due to pressure from the Secretary of War, Edwin Stanton. There was interesting testimony regarding Michael O'Laughlen, and how he was supposed to murder Secretary Stanton in his home the night of the assassination. He went to the home the night before and discovered that the Secretary was not home.[224] Why would he go there the night before if not to discuss with Secretary Stanton the assassination plot? It could be said he just wanted to view the front parlor, the butler, or maid to see what he was up against the next night.

This is conceivable, but why didn't he kill the Secretary the next night? Historians have said that he got "cold feet". Let's consider for a moment, that the real answer may be he never was supposed to kill the Secretary, but that Stanton's name was purposely added to the list of those to be killed in order to throw off any investigation. Secretary Stanton *(left)* then wanted

---

[223] America Unearthed Season 2 Episode 12.

[224] Doug Linder.

the conspirators to have hoods placed over their heads except for Mary Surratt and Doctor Samuel Mudd. [225] Why would Stanton make this request? One explanation would be that it is often difficult for some people to "look into the eyes of evil men"; especially the eyes of those involved in a plot to decapitate the United States government in a single night. Or, perhaps it was just a simple measure to keep co-conspirators from making eye contact, having someone panic in their final moments, and thereby "telling" too much. Lafayette Baker, the investigator of the crime and the man that tracked down Booth, gave congressional testimony that he had given Booth's personal diary to Secretary of War Stanton. Stanton denied having it in his possession for two years until public outcry and concern over a congressional investigation about the diary began to surface. [226]

Later, "In 1937, Otto Eisenschiml's, *Why Was Lincoln Murdered* was published. The book espoused the hypothesis that Secretary of War Edwin Stanton was directly involved in Lincoln's death. It alleged that Stanton was against Lincoln's mild Reconstruction policies and wanted him out of office so a more radical Reconstructionist policy could be employed." [227]

Why would Secretary Stanton want to conceal that he had the diary? The only logical explanation was that there was incriminating evidence in that diary;

---

[225] Doug Linder.

[226] O'Reilly, 274-278.

[227] "Lincoln Assassination Theories," accessed December 5, 2013, http://rogerjnorton.com/Lincoln74.html.

perhaps of meetings with Stanton and others within the Confederate Secret Service Bureau. The shadiness of Secretary of War Edwin Stanton's actions surrounding the assassination plot appear to be just coincidental.

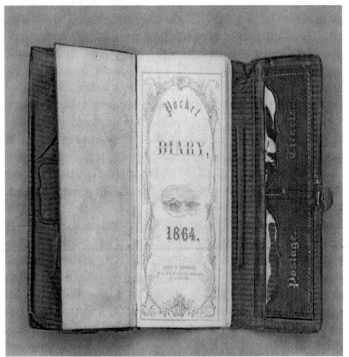

Photo of John Wilkes Booth's diary.
Courtesy Carol M. Highsmith.

"We're all stories, in the end."
– Doctor Who

The Confederate government envisioned and approved the operation referred to as, *Operation Come Retribution.* This operation entailed kidnapping and holding President Lincoln until the demands of the Confederate States of America were met. All are in agreement that it was a desperate plan to act upon; but as it is said, desperate times call for desperate measures. The lone assassin of the President of the United States of America was in fact carrying out the operational plan, but with slight modifications to how it was to be carried out based on his own ambition. Here is a ***theory*** of how the operation went from a kidnapping to an assassination.

John Wilkes Booth was at the Canadian Bureau station house in Montreal when he was introduced to John H. Surratt. Surratt had heard of the famous actor many times in the United States, and Booth knew of the Surratt family boarding house in Washington City. The two, along with other Canadian agents, were given a briefing by Jacob Thompson and Clement Clay on *Operation Come Retribution*; the plan to kidnap Lincoln, hold him for ransom, and bring an end to hostilities between the two nations. This plan had been approved by President Jefferson Davis. There was, though, an older gentleman that also spoke with Booth about his failed prior attempts at getting to the President, Doctor Luke Pryor Blackburn. Blackburn explained to Booth his plan to bring the deadly yellow fever disease to the Northern States, and apparently it had worked in the Union occupied city of New Bern, NC *(which was just a freak occurrence)*.

Booth listened intensively as Blackburn explained in great detail the issue he had to deal with logistically. The issues that plagued Blackburn logistically would not hinder the men chosen to carry out the operation. They were going to use the Richmond Line to smuggle the president out of

Washington, and into Confederate occupied territory. The plan did not call for the assassination of any government officials; although if it could be done without any hiccups, the other high value individuals (HVIs) to include; Secretary of State William H. Seward, Vice President Andrew Johnson, and Secretary of War Edwin Stanton, should be taken as well. The men understood their job and made their way back to their respective area of operations.

The Confederate agents waited for the approval of the Confederate government to carry out the plan. This would come via the Richmond Line to the commander of the operation, John Wilkes Booth. Being a famous stage actor, with access to the hierarchy of Washington, made Booth the obvious choice. He used the Surratt house as a staging base of operations, or safe house, and conducted detailed briefings of the routes and actions of each individual operator with contingencies. Booth also checked in with those on the Richmond Line that were a part of the plan to ensure that there was nothing that would hinder mission success. A major player for the agents was Doctor Samuel Mudd, who could move up and down the countryside conducting detailed reconnaissance of the area to ensure Union patrols would not come across their path; his natural reassuring title of "doctor" enabling his freedom of movement.

Another member of the Richmond Line that Booth had yet to meet was James W. Pumphrey, a livery owner in Washington D.C. Once introduced to Pumphrey by Surratt, Booth arranged for him to have his very best horses on standby if at all possible when the word came from Richmond for the operation to be initiated. All was set and ready to go.

Chapter 9 I am the Senate

The planning had been conducted and now all that was needed was the final approval of the mission from Richmond. A Confederate Agent in the highest echelons of the United States government was to send word to Richmond when the mission should take place. This man knew when the time was right because he had direct access to the President of the United States, and this man was Secretary of War Edwin Stanton.

The fires in New York City that were planned out and conducted by the Canadian Bureau could have ended the life of the commander of *Operation Come Retribution;* since Booth was at the Winter Garden Playhouse acting out a play with his siblings. This more than likely infuriated Booth because a mission like that conducted prior to Operation Come Retribution was not part of the entire plan. These operations were supposed to be conducted as simultaneous actions to cause the most confusion and panic amongst the populace and officials of the United States government. However, those actions had the exact opposite effect. Further, it caused some discontent for Booth who was still attempting to hold those in his operation together and convince them that soon they will receive word to commence the operation. This all changed on 9 April, 1865, when General Robert E. Lee surrendered the forces of the Army of Northern Virginia to General Ulysses S. Grant. Booth was convinced that the operation would never occur, and the Confederate States of America would be under the subjugation of the Union. The operation must happen soon if there was any hope for the Confederacy.

A monumental decision concerning the operation is made by Booth; it is changed from a kidnapping to an assassination. A message is sent to Secretary of War Edwin Stanton concerning the operation. He is informed that Booth received a message from Richmond to commence, and Stanton needs to ensure that Lincoln and others would be accessible. Booth left out the detail that he had decided to change the mission from kidnapping to assassination. On the night of 14 April, 1865, John Wilkes Booth's revised plan of *Operation Come Retribution* was conducted. Once the mission was over and the "conspirators" were captured, Secretary of War Edwin Stanton had their heads covered with hoods. He had this done because he could not stand to see those that had changed the plan and murdered the President of the United States, and attempted to take the lives of others within the United States government. It was supposed to be a kidnapping, not a murder.

"Words have no power to impress the mind without the exquisite horror of their reality."
– Edgar Allan Poe

Although based on facts, the theory articulated is purely circumstantial. However, certain weighty pieces of evidence which are normally neglected for want of popularity, state that: (1) The Confederacy had a Secret Service unit that conducted clandestine, covert, and overt operations; (2) the plan wasn't just John Wilkes Booth's; (3) President Jefferson Davis wasn't the "puppet master" and mastermind behind the entire plan; (4) the possibility that there were those in the Union government that wanted Lincoln out of the picture, therefore aided Confederate agents; and (5) that the highest echelons of the Union government contained actual members of pro-South organizations. It is hard for people to come to terms, or face the facts that what one is told on an everyday basis concerning history, is not necessarily always the truth.

President Lincoln's Box at Ford's Theater, April 1865. Courtesy the National Archives.

Lincoln's chair at Ford's Theater. National Archives

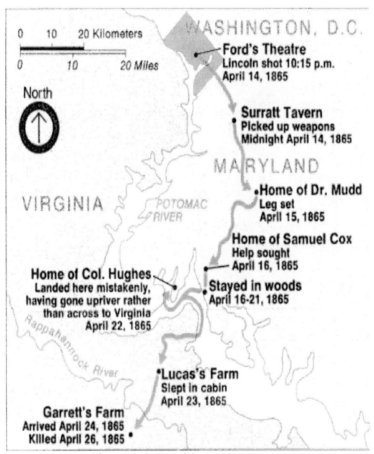

Figure 9-1. Booth's Escape Route.

The Conspirators. (1)David Herold, (2) George Atzerodt,
(3) Lewis Powell; (4) John Wilkes Booth.

Chapter 10
We Are the Last,
So Let's Be the Best

*"Now this is not the end. It is not even the
beginning of the end. But it is, perhaps, the end
of the beginning."*
– Winston Churchill

As time would tell, the Confederate Secret Service
Bureau, Special and Detached Services, and Signal
Corp would come to an abrupt end, but not all would
be lost, as would be expected. Much of their
operations, organizational structure, with its
accompanying leadership, would be lost forever, if it
weren't for the hard work and diligence of Civil War
history "buffs".

Simply examining the legislative records of the
Confederate Congress has left most studying this
topic of history, a distorted view of these
organizations. To be completely honest, many
historians today are captive to a centralized, "top
down" way of thinking. After all, as they reason, how
could agents and operatives perform actions prior to
the "official" establishment of the activity by the
centralized government? An excellent example of this
would be the legislation before the Confederate
Congress, while in "secret session" to create the
Bureau of Polytechnics, which had already long been
established. There are two primary reasons why we
see this occur often in the Confederate States. First,
the very structure of the CSA, with its strong
emphasis of State's rights and individual sovereignty,
resulted in more of a "bottom up" decision making

structure, with Congress's limited role, a mere function to formalize and fund that which had already been decided by the people. Second, the fledgling nation was at war, and certainly wasn't afforded the luxury of waiting on the deliberations of omniscient political leaders sitting in the smoke filled rooms of Richmond to make decisions affecting the very survival of the South.

It was a period of history, and especially during a time of war, when military leaders, along with their civilian counterparts, took action on their own, then asked their congressional leaders for approval and funding. Again, we see this in March of 1865, when the Confederate Congress approved the implementation and funding for the Special and Secret Service Bureau. The SSB had existed for quite some time and was the scourge of the Union Army. When Congress was considering this legislation in early 1865, the SSB consisted of four people "officially" working out of the main office in Richmond; Major Norris, Lieutenant Schley, Sergeant Gresham, and Private Charles Elisha Taylor.[228]

Of all these men, the latter, Private Taylor wrote down his experiences in the Signal Corps and some of the operations that he was able to observe. Charles Elisha Taylor was born on 28 October 1842 in Richmond, VA. Attending Richmond College at the age of only fifteen, he left school and saw it his duty to serve the Confederacy in order to defend his State, enlisting in the Confederate Army. Eventually, he was transferred to his post in Richmond where he observed awesome sights and heard stories too extravagant to be, though, were true. He survived the

---

[228] Taylor, 24.

war and made something of himself. Charles E. Taylor, the private, became Dr. Charles E. Taylor, the professor, linguist, minister, and future President of Wake Forest College. During his tenure as the President of Wake Forest College, he expanded the university and made it what it is to this day; and is remembered as such.[229] The following is from his personal account of what he remembered in the Signal Corps during those times, once Richmond fell, and more importantly, what he recalled after Booth shot Lincoln.

"A full and detailed account of the services of the Signal Corps in conducting secret correspondence through and beyond our lines would be the most romantic and interesting history. Part of this can never be written, for most of the actors have passed from the stage, leaving no record. And part, in its details, one would not like to assume the responsibility of writing...Mr. DeLeon was mistaken when he wrote that the system (referring to the spy network from Washington City, Maryland, and Richmond) was organized "late in the war". As a matter of fact, it was in full operation in 1862, the second year of the war...Perhaps the most useful of all the men connected with the C.S. Secret Service was Mr. Thomas A. Jones of Maryland...Not only Mr. Jones, but all his neighbors were in hearty sympathy with the South. Hence, this became the chief point of junction between the routes of agents in the North and couriers in the South...In addition to these, a detachment of troops (Union soldiers) were stationed

[229] William S. Powell, "Charles Elisha Taylor," Dictionary of North Carolina Biography Volume 6, last modified 1996, http://www.wfu.edu/history/HST_WFU/taylor.htm.

at Pope's Creek and another on Major Watson's (Mary Watson's husband) place not 300 yards from Mr. Jones' house.

But none of these precautions availed against the audacity and cunning of the Confederate agents...It was Mr. Jones who helped John Wilkes Booth to cross the Potomac River five days after the assassination of President Lincoln. This fact he was able to keep a secret for nearly twenty years...(newspaper articles) were written for the purposes of molding public opinion adversely to the continuance of the war and for other more specific purposes...urging that the United States Government should make peace before the Confederate army should receive reinforcement... In the great conflagration at the time of the evacuation of Richmond, the Signal office was destroyed and with it the invaluable copies of dispatches received and sent. The Signal and Secret Service of the Confederate States and its work are now only memories..." [230]

Dr. Charles Elisha Taylor

"I would try to convince you, but everything I have to say has already crossed your mind."
– Professor James Moriarty

Once Richmond fell, so did the foundation of the Secret Service Bureau and subsequent organizations. President Jefferson Davis made a run for it, refusing to accept defeat, hoping the Confederacy would be able to pull off a miracle. President Jefferson Davis with other refugees from Richmond that included Francis Lubbock and John H. Reagan, both of which hailed from Texas, joined in the hiding game, hoping

---

[230] Taylor, 18-24.

to avoid capture by Federal troops. As with the fate of one nation being dominated by another, on 10 May, 1865, in Irwinville, GA, President Davis along with the remainder of his cabinet, were arrested by Federal cavalrymen. His coachman, James Jones sounded the warning alarm, a gun shot, but it was too late and they were encircled. The group was plundered and the commanding Federal officer did nothing to stop it. The only person that was allowed to keep their money was Francis Lubbock, former Texas governor, because of the fight he put up to keep it.[231]

Even though Jefferson Davis was captured, what is interesting to note is that Francis Lubbock was with Jefferson Davis, why? Lubbock was the former governor of Texas, his brother, a former and famous Texas Ranger and commander of Terry's Rangers. Could the reason possibly have something to do with the long held belief that the KGC hid vast amounts of funds throughout the south and southwest portions of the Confederacy? Perhaps Lubbock was with Davis as they made their way deeper into the Confederacy because he knew the locations of the caches. Remember, there was a great deal of KGC activity in Texas while Lubbock was governor. Therefore, to ensure the survival of the Confederate Republic, Lubbock may have traveled with Davis in order to make funds available, along with Reagan, a colleague from Texas. Some things may never be known.

What is known, however, is that many of the names and faces involved in the Confederate's Secret Services have been forever lost to history, along with

---

[231] Michael B. Ballard, *A Long Shadow: Jefferson Davis and the Final Days of the Confederacy*, (Athens, GA: The University of Georgia Press, 1997), 141-143.

the fantastic stories they could have passed on, if it weren't for fear of visiting the gallows. These were the stories and tales of daring exploits of spies and saboteurs. Their primary purpose, of course, to end the war and preserve their beloved Confederacy; working tirelessly, providing information and creating and building devices of wonder, so that no more blood would have to be spilled on the soil of the North American continent.

Fortunately, for the special operations units that would follow, many of the Confederate Secret Service's tactics, techniques and procedures weren't lost. These secret organizations blazed a trail, laying the groundwork for the way future special operation forces were to be organized, trained, and operate. Their covert, overt, clandestine, subversion and sabotage missions have become the life force of many of the special operation forces around the world today, performing many of the same types of missions today, that the Confederates conducted on the Union decades earlier, albeit with modern advances.

"A serene spot along the Natchez Trace...on a tree-lined hill past Tupelo, Mississippi, stands a semi-circle of thirteen headstones bearing the words **UNKNOWN CONFEDERATE SOLDIER** *Fallen Warriors unknown to man, yet they are known to God.*

What brought you here' O' gallant men in grey? Were you at Shiloh, 'neath the blooms of April's peach orchard? Tired and wounded, you found a rest place at a spot on this tranquil hill, under these weathered stones which reads **UNKNOWN CONFEDERATE SOLDIER.**

Southern heroes all, but unknown to man- yet known to God.

Rest you brave fighting soul, fallen warriors in gray.
You served a cause noble and true, defending your native soil against an enemy in blue.

Rest on... **UNKNOWN CONFEDERATE SOLDIER** *though you're still unknown to man, you shall always be known to God."*[232]

---

[232] Allen Baswell, "Thirteen Headstones on a Hill," *Confederate Veteran,* September/October 2014, 23.

Appendix

*Photographs of Key Individuals of the Confederate
Secret Service Bureau, Special and Detached Service
and Signal Corps, and Secret Navy.*

Jacob Thompson
Former US Secretary
of Interior

Captain Thomas H. Hines
Former Morgan scout,
recruiter: Ohio, Indiana,
and Illinois.

**Robert Cobb
Kennedy**

**John Yates
Beall**

**Dr. Samuel
Mudd**

**Clement
Clay**

Sen. Henry Willson
of Massachusetts

Sen. Joseph Lane
of Oregon

Bibliography

Baswell, Allen. "Thirteen Headstones on a Hill," *Confederate Veteran,* September/October 2014.

Ballard, Michael B. A long Shadow: *Jefferson Davis and the Final Days of the Confederacy.* Athens, GA: The University of Georgia Press, 1997.

Powell, William S. "Charles Elisha Taylor," *Dictionary of North Carolina Biography Volume 6.* Last modified 1996. http://www.wfu.edu/history/HST_WFU/taylor.htm.

"Lincoln Assassination Theories." Accessed December 5, 2013. http://rogerjnorton.com/Lincoln74.html.

Kauffman, Michael W. *John Wilkes Booth and the Lincoln Conspiracies.* New York: Random House, 2004.

O'Reilly, Bill and Dwight Jon Zimmerman. *Lincoln's Last Days: The Shocking Assassination that Changed America Forever.* New York: Square Fish, 2014.

The Pumphrey Family Book. The Pumphrey Press, Vol. 2, No. 2. July 1980.

"Civil War Timeline." Accessed December 21, 2014. http://www.nps.gov/gett/historyculture/civil-war-timeline.htm.

Moon, Tom. Loyal and Lethal Ladies of Espionage. Bloomington, IN: iUniverse, 2000.

Rains, Gabriel J. and Peter S. Michie. *Confederate Torpedoes: Two Illustrated* 19th Century Works with New Appendices and Photographs. Jefferson, NC: McFarland, 2011.

Bibliography

"USS Cairo Gunboat and Museum." Accessed December 21, 2013. http://www.nps.gov/vick/u-s-s-cairo-gunboat.htm.

Wideman, John C. *The Sinking of the USS Cairo.* Jackson, MS: University Press of Mississippi, 2004.

"Online Library of Selected Images: U.S. Navy Ships, USS Cairo." Accessed September 121, 2013. http://www.history.navy.mil/photos/sh-usn/usnsh-c/cairo.htm.

"EX PARTE VALLANDIGHAM." Accessed 25 November 2014. http://www.oyez.org/cases/1851-1900/1863/1863_2.

"Clement Vallandigham." Accessed 25 November 2014. http://www.ohiohistorycentral.org/w/Clement_Vallandigham.

Tucker, Spencer C. *American Civil War: The Definitive Encyclopedia and Document Collection.* Santa Barbara, CA: ABC-CLIO, 2013.

Lonn, Ella. *Foreigners in the Confederacy.* Chapel Hill: UNC Press Books, 2002.

Henry, Mike. *What They Didn't Teach You in American History Class.* Boulder, CO: R&L Education, 2014.

Miller, Francis Trevelyan and Robert Sampson Lanier. *Soldier life, Secret Service.* New York: Review of Reviews Company, 1912.

"Brigadier General Gabriel J. Rains: Father of Modern Mine Warfare." Accessed 2 August 2014. http://gabrielrains.com/confederate-service/.

Bibliography

Pippen, Craig. "Gabriel James Rains Bio-Sketch." Camp 2205, Stem, NC. Last modified January 2014. http://www.ncscv.org/gabriel-james-rains.

"Commander Hunter Davidson, Confederate States Navy." Accessed February 9, 2014. http://www.history.navy.mil/photos/pers-us/uspers-d/h-davdsn.htm.

"Thomas Edgeworth Courtenay." Accessed February 9, 2014. http://scourt.tempdomainname.com/tec.htm.

Annual Reports of the Navy Department for the Fiscal Year by United States. Navy Department

Smithsonian Channel, "America's Lost Submarine." Released 2010.

"NavSource Online: Submarine Photo Archive Pioneer." Accessed February 15, 2013. http://www.navsource.org/archives/08/08448.htm.

Dash, Mike. "The Amazing (If True) Story of the Submarine Mechanic Who Blew Himself Up Then Surfaced as a Secret Agent for Queen Victoria, The leading mechanic of the famed H.L. Hunley led quite the life, if we can believe any of it." Last modified June 30, 2014. http://www.smithsonianmag.com/history/amazing-if-true-story-submarine-mechanic-who-blew-himself-then-surfaced-secret-agent-queen-victoria-180951905/?no-ist.

"Journal of the Congress of the Confederate States of America, 1861 to 1865 Volume 6."Confederate States of America Congress.

Baird, Nancy Disher. *Luke Pryor Blackburn: Physician, Governor, Reformer*. Lexington, KY: The University of Kentucky Press, 1979.

Bibliography

"Camp Douglas Conspiracy of 1864: The Northwestern Confederacy." Accessed July 7, 2013. http://campdouglas.compuliance.com/camp-douglas-conspiracy-of-1864-the-northwestern-confederacy/.

Owsley Sr., Frank L. *King Cotton Diplomacy: Foreign Relations of the Confederate States of America.* Tuscaloosa, AL: University Alabama Press, 2008.

"Clay to Texas Senator Louis Wingfall, April 29, 1864." The Clays of Alabama. Lexington: University of Kentucky Press, 1958.

Case, Lynn M. and Warren F. Spencer. The United States and France Civil War Diplomacy. Philadelphia: University of Pennsylvania Press, 1970.

"The Index 1863". Accessed on April 14, 2013. http://www.bl.uk/onlinegallery/onlineex/uscivilwar/high lights/theindex/theindex16july63.html.

Thomas, Emory M. *The Confederate Nation: 1861-1865.* New York: First Harper Perennial Edition Published, 2011.

Palmer, Vera "Honest John' Letcher, War Governor From Tailor's Bench to Old Dominion's Executive Mansion Is Romance of Little Known, Much Loved Virginian." Richmond Times-Dispatch (Richmond, VA), January 13, 1935.

Steers, Edward. *Blood on the Moon: The Assassination of Abraham Lincoln.* Lexington, KY: The University Press of Kentucky, 2005.

"America Unearthed Season 2 Episode 12." History Channel. Released February 15, 2014.

Bibliography

The War of the Rebellion: v. 1-8 [serial no. 114-121]
Correspondence. Orders by United States War
Department.

Eggleston, Larry G. *Women in the Civil War: Extraordinary
Stories of Soldiers, Spies, Nurses, Doctors, Crusaders, and
Others.*
Jefferson, NC: McFarland & Company Inc., 2009.

"Kentucky: A History of the State, Perrin, Battle, Kniffin,
8th ed., 1888,
Jefferson Co." Accessed July 21, 2013.
http://www.rootsweb.ancestry.com/~kygenweb/kybiog/je
fferson/robinson.s.txt.

Mayers, Adam. *Dixie & the Dominion: Canada, the
Confederacy, and the War for the Union.* Toronto: Dundurn
Press, 2003.

"Notorious Terrorist Attacks in New York City." Accessed
September 18, 2013.
http://www.newyorktalksandwalks.com/nm/publish/new
s_42.html.

Roberts, Sam. "As Booth Brothers Held Forth, 1864
Confederate Plot Against New York Fizzled." Last modified
November 24, 2014.
http://www.nytimes.com/2014/11/25/nyregion/as-
booth-brothers-held-forth-1864-confederate-plot-against-
new-york-fizzled.html?_r=1.

Rosenhek, Jackie. "The beginnings of bioterrorism,"
During the Civil War, Dr. Blackburn hatched a plan to use
sickness as a weapon. Last modified August 2008.
http://www.doctorsreview.com/history/the-beginnings-of-
bioterrorism/.

Bibliography

"Yellow Fever." Accessed October 12, 2013. http://www.mayoclinic.org/diseases-conditions/yellow-fever/basics/definition/con-20032263.

Van Doren Stern, Philip. *Secret Missions of the Civil War.* New York: Bonanza Books, 1987.

"Intelligence in the Civil War." cia.gov. Last modified January 03, 2012. https://www.cia.gov/library/publications/additional-publications/civil-war/p5.htm.

Linder, Doug. "The Trial of the Lincoln Assassination Conspirators." Last modified January 1, 2009. http://law2.umkc.edu/faculty/projects/ftrials/lincolncon spiracy/lincolnaccount.html.

"The Confederacy's Bomb Brothers." *National Mine Action Center* Issue 6.1. jmu.edu. Last modified April 2002. http://www.jmu.edu/cisr/journal/6.1/notes/robbins/rob bins.htm.

Marrin, William J. "Thomas Jordan." June 11th, 1896. Last Modified November 27, 2010. http://penelope.uchicago.edu/Thayer/E/Gazetteer/Place s/America/United_States/Army/USMA/AOG_Reunions/2 7/Thomas_Jordan*.html.

Gaddy, David Winfred. "William Norris - and the Confederate Signal and Secret Service." Last modified January 1, 2014. http://mdscv.org/1398/Norrisbio.htm.

Crowley, R.O. "The Confederate Torpedo Service." *The Century Illustrated Monthly Magazine,* Volume 56 (1898): 290-300.

Tidwell, William A. *April '65: Confederate Covert Action in the American Civil War.* Kent, OH: The Kent State University, 1995.

Bibliography

"Rose O'Neal Greenhow - Confederate Spy." Accessed August 14, 2014. http://www.ourarchives.wikispaces.net/Rose+O%27Neal+Greenhow+-+Confederate+Spy#The%20Civil%20War-Senator%20Henry%20Wilson.

"Rose O'Neal Greenhow - Confederate Spy." Accessed August 14, 2014. http://www.ourarchives.wikispaces.net/Rose+O%27Neal+Greenhow+-+Confederate+Spy.

Bakeless, John. *Spies of the Confederacy*. New York: Dover Publications, 2011.

Wilson, Camilla J. *Civil War Spies*. New York: Scholastic Inc., 2010.

FM 1-02 (FM 101-5-1) Operational Terms and Graphics. Headquarters Department of the Army, 2004.

Pavlovsky, Arnold. *Riding in Circles J.e.b. Stuart and the Confederate Cavalry 1861-1862*. New York: Arnold M. Pavlovsky Publishing, 2010.

Markle, Donald E. *Spies and Spymasters of the Civil War*. New York: Hippocrene Books, 1994.

"Belle Boyd". Accessed August 14, 2014. http://www.nps.gov/resources/person.htm?id=47.

Jones, J. William. "The Signal Corps in the Confederate States Army," Southern Historical Society Papers, Volume 16. Accessed January 30, 2014, http://www.perseus.tufts.edu/hopper/text?doc=Perseus:text:2001.05.0273:chapter=1.11.

Bibliography

Jones, J. William. "The Signal Corps in the Confederate States Army," *Southern Historical Society Papers*, Volume 16. Accessed January 30, 2014, http://www.perseus.tufts.edu/hopper/text?doc=Perseus %3Atext%3A2001.05.0273%3Achapter%3D1.11.

Blair, John F. *Gray Phantoms of the Cape Fear: Running the Civil War Blockade.* Winston-Salem, NC: John F. Blair, 1998.

Hammersley & Cowardin. "The Daily Dispatch: June 5, 1862." Southern Historical Society Papers, Accessed January 30, 2014, http://www.perseus.tufts.edu/hopper/text?doc=Perseus %3Atext%3A2006.05.0493.

Still, Kathy. "Partisan Rangers Act had unintended consequences, Civil War expert contends." Last modified September 26, 2014, http://www.uvawise.edu/News/Partisan-Rangers-Act-had-unintended-consequences-Civil-War-expert-contends.

Hatley, Allen G. *Early Texas Indian Wars, 1822-1835.* Honolulu, HI: Talei Publications, 2005.

Cox, Mike. *The Texas Rangers: Wearing the Cinco Peso 1821-1900.* New York: Forge Books, 2008.

Brown, John Henry. "Defeat of Comanches and Wacos on Peach Creek ca. 1838." The Indian Wars and Pioneers of Texas. Accessed August 23, 2014, http://www.tamu.edu/faculty/ccbn/dewitt/indiantales.ht m.

"Terry's Texas Rangers." Accessed September 24, 2014, http://www.bbcwr.us/8th_texas_cavalry.html.

Bibliography

McAfee, Michael *J. Don Troiani's Regiments and Uniforms of the Civil War*. Mechanicsburg, PA: Stackpole Books, 2014.

Cutrer, Thomas W. "EIGHTH TEXAS CAVALRY: TERRY'S TEXAS RANGERS," Handbook of Texas Online. Accessed May 14, 2014. Modified on March 4, 2011. (http://www.tshaonline.org/handbook/online/articles/qk e02) Published by the Texas State Historical Association.

Campbell, Randolph B. "KNIGHTS OF THE GOLDEN CIRCLE," Handbook of Texas Online. Accessed May 14, 2014. Uploaded on September 19, 2010. (http://www.tshaonline.org/handbook/online/articles/vb k01)Published by the Texas State Historical Association.

Jones, R. Steven. "Our Trust is in the God of Battles: The Civil War Letters of Robert Franklin Bunting, Chaplain, Terry's Texas Rangers, C.S.A." Accessed September 15, 2014, http://muse.jhu.edu/journals/swh/summary/v111/111. 2.jones.html.

Bailey, Anne. *Between the Enemy and Texas: Parsons's Texas Cavalry in the Civil War*. College Station, TX: Texas A&M University Press, 2013.

United States War Department. *The War of the Rebellion: A Compilation of the Official Records of the Union and Confederate Armies.* Washington D.C.: Government Printing Office, 1901.

Tidwell, William A. *Come Retribution: The Confederate Secret Service and the Assassination of Lincoln.* Jackson, MS: The University Press of Mississippi, 1988.

"H.L. Hunley," accessed March 5, 2013, http://www.sonofthesouth.net/leefoundation/h-l-hunley-submarine.htm.

Bibliography

"Friends of the Hunley First Crew." Accessed March 5, 2013, http://hunley.org/main_index.asp?CONTENT=FIRSTCRE W.

"Friends of the Hunley First Crew." Accessed March 5, 2013, http://hunley.org/main_index.asp?CONTENT=SECONDC REW.

"Spies and Conspiracy." Accessed June 12, 2014. http://www.ourarchives.wikispaces.net/Spies+and+Cons piracy.

"Jedburghs." Accessed December 14, 2013. http://www.soc.mil/OSS/jedburghs.html.

Get Lost In Loudon. "Hunting the Grey Ghost." YouTube video. Accessed June 7, 2013.

Mitchell, Reid. *Civil War Soldiers: Their Expectations and Their Experiences*. New York: Penguin Books, 1988.

Hester, Robert. "Descriptions of Confederate Combat Units Enlisted in Hyde County, North Carolina." Accessed February, 2 2014.

US Navy. Civil War Warfare Documentary. YouTube video. Accessed June 7, 2013.

de Kay, James Tertuis. *The Rebel Raiders: The Astonishing History of the Confederacy's Secret Navy*. New York: The Random House Publishing Group, 2002.

Bulloch, James Dunwody. *The Secret Service of the Confederate States in Europe*. New York: G.P. Putnam's Sons, 1884.

Bibliography

Burnett, Lonnie A. Confederate Propagandist: Selected on Revolution. Tuscaloosa, AL: University Alabama Press, 2008.

"Greek Fire." Accessed April 4, 2013. http://www.britannica.com/EBchecked/topic/244571/Greek-fire.

"Greenhow Obituary." Wilmington Sentinel. 1 October 1864.

Taylor, Charles Elisha. The Signal and Secret Service of the Confederate States. Hamlet, NC: Capital Printing CO., 1903.

Smith, Richard Harris. *OSS: The Secret History of America's First Central Intelligence Agency.* Guildford, CT: First Lyons Press, 2005.

Spencer C. Tucker, *American Civil War: The Definitive Encyclopedia and Document Collection,* (Santa Barbara, CA: ABC-CLIO, 2013), 913-914.

Jane Singer, *The Confederate Dirty War,* (Jefferson, NC: McFarland & Company, Inc., 2005) 82-83.

David C. Keehn, *Knights of the Golden Circle: Secret Empire, Southern Secession, Civil War,* (Baton Rouge, Louisiana State University Press, 2013) 8-9.

John C. Wideman, *The Sinking of the USS Cairo,* (Jackson, MS, University Press of Mississippi, 2004) 17.

Glossary

Glossary

Glossary

Glossary

CPSIA information can be obtained at www.ICGtesting.com
Printed in the USA
BVOW03s2131120415

395395BV00004B/2/P